Write in Style

Fourth Edition

A Guide to
the Short Term Paper

by
Edward P. Von der Porten

Style conforms to the
MLA Handbook
for Writers of Research Papers,
Sixth Edition, 2003.

Senior Editor: Gay Russell-Dempsey

Book Design: Deborah L. Bell

Reviewers: Bob Kaczor
Newark High School, Newark, Ohio

Claudia Anne Katz
Highland Middle School, Libertyville, Illinois

Gretchen Kauffman
Des Moines Public Schools, Des Moines, Iowa

Sue Ann Kuby
Highland Middle School, Libertyville, Illinois

Fourth Edition Copyright © 2006 Perfection Learning® Corporation
Third Edition Copyright © 1998 Perfection Learning® Corporation
Second Edition Copyright © 1988 Perfection Form® Corporation
First Edition Copyright © 1976 Perfection Form® Corporation

For information, contact
Perfection Learning® Corporation
1000 North Second Avenue, P.O. Box 500
Logan, Iowa 51546-0500.
Phone: 1-800-831-4190
Fax: 1-800-543-2745
perfectionlearning.com

#79984 ISBN 0-7891-6665-8

  2 3 4 5 6 PP 10 09 08 07 06

Table of Contents

Don't Do Anything Until You Read This!

Write in Style is the "how-to" book for effectively presenting your research reports. By following the guidelines for good structure and form, you will learn how to present your facts and ideas according to the conventions of scholarship. These practices will help you give any problem-solving project order and logic.

Step by step, this guide explains the mechanics of writing a formal term paper. It tells you how to organize materials—note cards, the outline, etc. It also tells you about presentation—rough and final drafts, acknowledgments, and formats.

Each detail is essential in creating a well-constructed paper. Pay careful attention to every step. Examples for each section show the format at work and offer further guidelines.

The complexities of form can be mastered with practice. Correct form helps you share the information you have gathered.

The Topic Card   1

Pointing the Way

The success of the term paper depends on a carefully defined topic. Selecting a topic requires considerable thought. Your teacher may suggest some broad topic areas for research. From these, it is up to you to choose a specific area you want to investigate. Make it something that interests you. The work will be much easier if you are motivated by real curiosity.

Within your scope of interest, plan a question about a specific issue or problem you want to investigate. Write the question on an index card. (See Fig. 1.) From this question, the main idea of your paper (the *thesis*) will emerge. See the examples below.

> William Czerwinski
> American History
> 8:00 MWF
>
> How did mass media influence the presidential election of 2004?

> Kathleen Carver
> American History
> Period Three
>
> What is the difference between child labor laws one hundred years ago and today?

Fig. 1. Topic Cards.

Reminders

- Keep the subject very limited in scope.
- Write a question, not a title.

Examples of good topics, all quite limited in scope	Examples of poor topics	Reasons topics don't work
☞ How did Edgar Lee Masters use real people in his *Spoon River Anthology*?	Characters in *The Spoon River Anthology*	This is not a question.
☞ What influence did Twain's river background have on his writing?	What happens on the Mississippi River in *The Adventures of Huckleberry Finn*?	No problem is stated; the paper would merely recount events.
☞ What themes run throughout S. E. Hinton's novels?	Who is S. E. Hinton?	This is not really a question, just an excuse for a biography.
☞ Did Rosalind Franklin face prejudice while researching DNA?	What did Rosalind Franklin discover?	Too easy.
☞ How did the Underground Railroad operate?	How has the Underground Railroad influenced life in our time?	Too difficult. Research material would probably be too hard to locate.
☞ What is global warming, and how do we stop it?	What is global warming?	Too broad. This needs an explanation and ideas for a resolution.

2 Source Cards

Spotlight on Sources

You must list every book, article, or other reference where you find information or background material for your paper. Teachers often require you to record these sources on 3"×5" index cards, or *source cards*. You may also, however, have the option of recording sources on a computer, preferably a laptop. As you compile your sources, enter all the information into your computer file. To correct stored entries or to add new sources to the list, retrieve the file, make the changes, and save the new file. You can print out this file at any time.

The method you use to record your sources is not as important as having the source clearly identified. (You'll acknowledge sources both within your paper and in a *works cited* section at the end of the paper.)

When should you record information from a source? After you decide a source has good information and before you take a single note. This habit will save you from having to retrace your steps later to find the missing information. Sources should always be listed accurately and completely.

What to Record

Before you take any notes from a source, record all of the following information:

- author(s)
- editor(s) or translator(s), if any
- title (including subtitle)
- edition (for instance, 4th or abridged)
- place published
- publisher
- date published
- page numbers, if you're using only one item from a larger work

(See Fig. 2.)

Sometimes you may conduct interviews or write letters or e-mail to get information. When you do, note the name of your source, the person's position, the type of correspondence, and the date of contact.

Abbreviating Publishers' Names

Shorten or abbreviate publishers' names whenever possible using the following rules:

- Use traditional abbreviations where appropriate.
- Leave out articles, business abbreviations, and descriptive words such as *Books*, *Press*, and *House*.

- Use only the last name of a company named for one person. (For example, *Knopf* instead of *Alfred A. Knopf, Inc.*)
- Use only the first name of a company named for more than one person. (For example, *Holt* for *Holt, Rinehart, and Winston, Inc.*)
- Use *U* and *P* for *University* and *Press* (*U of Illinois P*, for example).

Missing Information

If the place of publication or publisher is not shown in the work, indicate this lack of information. Write *n.p.*, which means *no place*, before the colon, or *n.p.*, which means *no publisher*, after the colon, in the appropriate place. (See Fig. 3.)

If the date of publication is not shown, write *n.d.*, meaning *no date*, in place of the date. If the material has no page numbers, write *n. pag.*, meaning *no paging*. (See Fig. 3.) Note: Capitalization of abbreviations will depend upon placement.)

If the author's name does not appear on the source material, begin the entry with the title (See Fig. 3.)

Source Card Formats

The next pages show how to do different types of source cards. You'll find explanations of each type in the wide columns and examples in the narrow columns.

The examples given in blue boxes under *Model* show the basic format for each type of card. The formats are arranged in the order you are most likely to need them. You won't need every form. Look up the forms as you need them.

Ogilvy, David. <u>Confessions of an Advertising Man</u>. London: Southbank, 2004.

Fig 2. Source cards for a book and an Internet site.

Chandran, K, et al. "Endosomal Proteolysis of the Ebola Virus Glycoprotein Is Necessary for Infection." Ed. James M. Cunningham. <u>Science</u> 14 Apr. 2005 <http://www.sciencemag.org/cgi/content/abstract/1110656v1>

<u>Drug Abuse: The Empty Life</u>. N.p.: n.p., n.d. N. pag.

Fig. 3. Source card with missing information.

Hints

If you make photocopies from a book, make a copy of the title page too. Write in the date of publication (usually found on the back of the title page). Write down the library call number in case you want to refer to the book again.

When you photocopy magazine articles, make sure that you have all of the information you need. If the article is continued, it's easy to miss the last page(s). Write your source card before you photocopy.

Books and Pamphlets

Model	Explanation

Model

Author's last name, First name. <u>Title of Book or Pamphlet: Including Subtitle</u>. City of publication: Publisher, date of publication.

Edition Information

Berkman, Robert I. <u>Find It Fast: How to Uncover Expert Information on Any Subject Online or in Print</u>. 5th ed. New York: HarperCollins, 2000.

Two Publishers

Chang, Ina. <u>A Separate Battle: Women and the Civil War</u>. New York: Penguin; Toronto: McClelland, 1991.

No Individual Author

<u>New York Public Library American History Desk Reference</u>. New York: MacMillan, 1997.

Translator

<u>Beowulf</u>. Trans. Burton Raffel. New York: Signet-Penguin, 1999.

Editors

Faulkner, William. <u>Country Lawyer and Other Stories for the Screen</u>. Eds. Louis Daniel Brodsky and Robert W. Hamblin. Jackson: U of Mississippi P, 1987.

Explanation

One Author

Most of your sources will probably be written by one author. (See Fig. 2.) To write the source card, look at the title page. Write the author's last name, followed by a comma, then the first name, followed by a period. Next, write the title (including any subtitle), underline it, and place a period after it. If the work has been revised or abridged, give the edition number or description next. Then add the city of publication, a colon, the publisher, a comma, and the date of publication. End with a period.

☞ You do not need to list any degrees that follow the author's name, but do include distinctions like *Jr.* or *III.*

☞ If more than one city is mentioned, give only the name of the first city mentioned. If more than one publisher is mentioned, list all publishers mentioned in the order given. Separate the publishers with a semicolon.

☞ Publishers often group books together under an imprint, such as Crime Club or Vintage. If you see an imprint on the title page, write the imprint, followed by a hyphen and the publisher's name; for example, Vintage-Random.

Author as Editor or Translator

When many editors have prepared different versions of a work for publication, mentioning the editor's name is one way to specify the edition you used. When a work has been translated into English, you should identify the translator.

First write the author's name (last name first), period, the title (underlined), and a period. If the author's name is not known, begin the entry with the title of the work.

Then write the abbreviation *Ed.* (for editor) or *Trans.* (for translator). Continue with the editor's or translator's name (first name first) and a period. Finally, write the city of publication, a colon, the publisher, a comma, the date of publication, and a period.

Explanation	Model
## Author of an Anthology You don't need to list all of the authors whose works are collected in an anthology. Begin the entry with the name(s) of the editor(s) who chose the different works.	**Anthology** Hong, Maria, ed. <u>Growing Up Asian American: An Anthology</u>. New York: Morrow, 1993.
## Multiple Authors If a work has two or three authors, list each author by name. Begin with the first author's last name, followed by a comma, then the first name, followed by a comma and the other authors' names. Give the remaining authors' names first name first. (See Fig. 4.) If a work has more than three authors, you may list all the authors or give the first author's name, followed by a comma and the words *et al.*	**Three Authors** Capinera, John L., Ralph D. Scott, and Thomas J. Walker. <u>Field Guide to Grasshoppers, Katydids, and Crickets of the United States</u>. Ithaca: Cornell UP, 2005. **Four or More Authors** Brickman, Rick, et al. <u>Dealing with People You Can't Stand: How to Bring Out the Best in People at Their Worst</u>. New York: McGraw-Hill, 2002. **Collaborators** X, Malcolm, with Alex Haley. <u>The Autobiography of Malcolm X</u>. New York: Grove, 1964.
## Corporate Author Sometimes the author credited is not an individual person, but a company, committee, or organization. If the corporate name is not included in the title, list the group as the author. If the corporate name is included in the title, begin with the title.	**Corporate Author's Name Not in Title** American Medical Women's Association. <u>Guide to Nutrition and Wellness</u>. New York: Dell, 1996. **Corporate Author's Name in Title** <u>Rodale Organic Gardening Solutions</u>. Emmaus: Rodale, 2000.
## Sacred Texts Cite sacred texts, such as the Bible or the Koran, as books; however, do not underline the title.	**Sacred Texts** The Revised English Bible Standard Text Edition. Cambridge: Cambridge UP, 2002.

> Capinera, John L., Ralph D. Scott, and Thomas J. Walker. <u>Field Guide to Grasshoppers, Katydids, and Crickets of the United States</u>. Ithaca: Cornell UP, 2005.

Fig. 4. Source card for a book with multiple authors.

☞ *The MLA Handbook* contains a list of abbreviations for books of the Bible.

Magazines and Newspapers

Model   *Explanation*

Popular Magazine Articles

Author's last name, First name. "Article Title." <u>Magazine Title</u> [day] month year: page numbers.

Bennett, Lerone, Jr.,"Harriet Tubman's Private War." <u>Ebony</u> Mar. 2005: 50B-50G.

- -

Sedgewick, John. "Junk Medicine—Sorting the Truth from the Trash." <u>Self</u> Aug. 1997: 144+.

Articles in Popular Magazines

Begin with the author's name (if known). Next write the title of the article in quotation marks, and add a period. Then write the magazine title and underline it. Finally, add the publication information. (Abbreviate any month that is more than four letters long.) After the date, put a colon, followed by the page number(s). End with a period.

☛ If no author is credited, begin with the title.

☛ Some magazine articles are broken into more than two sections. For example, an article might begin on page 5, continue on page 33, and end on page 39. In such cases, list the first page only and a plus sign (5+).

Academic Journal Articles

Author's last name, First name. "Article Title." <u>Magazine Title</u> volume. [issue number if the volume is not paginated continuously] (year of publication): beginning page–ending page [if consecutive].

Article in a Journal Paged Consecutively

Murphy, Richard. "Anorexia: The Cheating Disorder." <u>College English</u> (1996): 898–903.

- -

Article in a Journal Not Paged Consecutively

Stemer, Michael. "Closing the Gate: The Persian Gulf War Revisited." <u>Current History</u> 96 (1997): 13–19.

Articles in Scholarly Journals

Why are there different formats for popular and academic magazines? To look up popular magazines like *Sports Illustrated* or *Glamour,* all you need to know is the date of publication. Academic journals are bound by volume, so you also need to know the volume and issue number.

How can you tell which format to use? Popular magazines provide general background information. Academic or scholarly journals are written for experts. When in doubt, write down everything you might need: date of publication and volume, issue, and page numbers.

☛ Use the scholarly format if a magazine

- is published by a university
- has no ads for commercial products
- numbers pages consecutively throughout the year
- is indexed in specialized academic indexes such as the *Social Sciences and Humanities Index*

Newspaper Article

Author's last name, First name. "Article Title." <u>Newspaper Title</u> [city of publication if not in title] day month year, edition (or section): page information.

Articles in Newspapers

If the article has a byline, begin with the author's name. Give the article title in quotation marks, followed by a period. Then write the name of the newspaper and underline it. If the city in which the paper is published is not in the title, give the name of the city enclosed in brackets; for example, <u>Globe and Mail</u> [Toronto]. Use no punctuation between the name of the newspaper and the date of publication. Put a colon after the date, followed by section and page information.

☞ Omit introductory articles such as *the* in a newspaper's name. If the paper has more than one edition, give the edition after the date. Also include the section number and page number(s) (6 Jan. 2006, late ed., sec. 4: 34+).

☞ You need not cite the city of publication for nationally published newspapers.

Articles in Newspapers (cont'd)

Hymowitz, Carol. "The Perils of Picking CEOs." Wall Street Journal 15 Mar. 2005: B1+.

- -

Bigness, Jon. "Cars Evolve into Rolling Computers." Chicago Tribune 15 Sept. 1997: B1+.

Editorials

Begin references to signed editorials with the author's name. If the editorial is unsigned, begin with the title. After the title, put the word *Editorial*, capitalized and followed by a period. End with the publication information.

Journal Editorial

Crispell, Diane. "Of Data Paralysis, Slugs, and TV Ratings." Editorial. American Demographics 19.3 (1997): 2.

- -

Newspaper Editorial

"Action on Land Mines." Editorial. Christian Science Monitor 16 Sept. 1997: 20.

Letters to the Editor

Begin with the author's name. If the letter has a title, write the title in quotation marks. Write *Letter*, followed by a period. Then give the publication information.

☞ Some letters may be written in reply to letters that have already been published. In that case, write *Reply to letter of (previous author's name)* instead of *Letter*.

Letter to the Editor in a Magazine

Reichman, Lee B. "The Kursk Syndrome." Letter. New Yorker 1 Nov. 2004: 8.

- -

Schneider, David. Reply to letter of William J. LeNoble and Charles S. Springer, Jr. Scientific American Oct. 1997: 8.

- -

Letter to the Editor in a Newspaper

Blazer, Gregory H. "Miss America More Than Swimsuit." Letter. USA Today 11 Sept. 1997: 14A.

Reviews

Begin references to signed reviews with the reviewer's name. If the review is unsigned but has a title, begin with the title. If the review is unsigned and untitled, begin with *Rev. of*. Then write the title of the work reviewed, followed by a comma, the word *by* and the author's name, and publication information.

☞ If more than one work is reviewed, separate the titles by commas. Place the word *and* in front of the final title.

☞ If the work is by someone other than an author—an editor, translator, or director, for example—use the abbreviation *ed.*, *trans.*, or *dir.*, as appropriate.

☞ When citing a review of a film or theatre work, add information about the production.

Review in a Magazine

Brooke, David. Rev. of John Wayne's America: The Politics of Celebrity, by Garry Wills. Commentary July 1997: 59–60.

- -

Review of More Than One Work

Gornick, Vivian. "Lost in America." Rev. of Other People's Houses and Her First American, by Lore Segal. The Nation 13 Dec. 2004: 26–30.

- -

Review of a Film or Theatre Production

Schickel, Richard. "The Human Face of Evil." Rev. of Downfall, dir. Oliver Hirschbiegel. Time 21 Mar. 2005: 75.

Parts of a Whole

Model | *Explanation*

Hall, Michael. "Running for His Life." <u>Best American Sports Writing</u>. Ed. Richard Ben Cramer. New York: Houghton Mifflin, 2004. 272–85.

Articles from Anthologies

Write the name of the article's author (last name first), a period, the title (in quotation marks), and a period (inside the quotation marks). Follow with the title of the book, which should be underlined, and a period. Next write the abbreviation *Ed.* (or *Eds.*, for more than one editor) and the editor's name (first name first), followed by a period. Write the city of publication, a colon, the publisher, a comma, the date of publication, a period, page numbers, and a period.

Familiar Work

<u>Merriam-Webster's Collegiate Dictionary</u>. Unabridged. New York: Merriam-Webster, 2003.

"Holocaust." <u>New Standard Encyclopedia</u>. 2000 ed.

Signed Article

Brody, Jane. "Hypertension." <u>New York Times Guide to Essential Knowledge</u>. New York: St. Martin's, 2004.

Articles from Reference Works

Articles in reference works or entries in dictionaries follow the same general format as articles in an anthology. Editors' names, however, are not included. If entries are arranged alphabetically, you do not need to include page or volume numbers.

☞ For familiar reference works, especially those that are published every year, list only the edition (if applicable) and the year of publication. If a reference book has appeared in only one edition, provide complete publication information.

☞ If an article is signed, list the author's name before the article, last name first. (The name of the author of an encyclopedia article, usually follows the article. If only the author's initials are given, check the first volume for a list of authors.)

Multivolume Reference

Houston, Jeanne Wakatsuke. "Colors." <u>Contemporary American Autobiography Series</u>. Vol. 16. New York: Gale, 1972. 171–86.

Book with More Than One Volume

Deming, Robert H., ed. <u>James Joyce: The Critical Heritage</u>. 2 vols. London: Routledge, 1970.

Multiple Volume Works

One book in a multivolume work is handled in much the same way as a single volume. Include the number of the volume used after the title. Then give the publishing information for the volume. If you used more than one volume, give the total number of volumes in the work ("8 vols.") before the publication information.

Foreword

Terkel, Studs. Foreword. <u>Bridges of Memory: Chicago's First Wave of Black Migration</u>. By Timvel D. Black, Jr. Evanston: Northwestern U Press, 2003. ix–x.

A Foreword, Preface, or Afterword

When someone other than the author writes a foreword, preface, or afterword, begin with the name of the person writing the piece, followed by a period. Then write the kind of writing it is, followed by a period. Write the title and a period. Then write *By* and the author of the book, first name first. Follow with the place of publication, the publisher, date, and page numbers cited. If the writer of the piece is also the author of the book, use only the last name after *By*. If the text has a title, put it in quotes, then name the kind of writing.

Government Publications

Explanation

Official U.S. government publications cover almost every subject imaginable, from water pollution to auto crash tests. Government Web sites cover out-of-this-world subjects as well; you can view photos from space probes at several NASA-sponsored sites.

When you cite a government document, begin with the author's name, if known. If the author is not known, name the government that produced the document (for example, *California* or *United Nations*). Then give the name of the government agency that produced the document, followed by a period. Next comes the title, which is underlined. Relevant information about the document follows, separated by commas. Usually, all you will need is the type and number of the publication. For laws and Congressional hearings, however, include the bill or session number and the session of Congress.

☞ These abbreviations are helpful when referring to U.S. government publications.

> H.—House
> S.—Senate
> *Cong. Rec.*—*Congressional Record* (Underline this source, and give only the title, date, and page numbers.)
> Dept.—department
> Doc.—document
> GPO—Government Printing Office
> Rept.—report
> Res.—resolution, as in S. Res. 20
> Sess.—session

Model

> **Author's name, if known. Name of government agency. <u>Title</u>. Relevant information, such as the type and number of the publication. Place, publisher, and date of publication.**

Bulletin

United States. Dept. of Labor. <u>Occupational Outlook Handbook: 1994–95</u>. Bulletin 2450. Washington: GPO, 1994.

Legislation-in-process

United States. Cong. Senate. "Right-to-Know-More and Pollution Prevention Act of 1997." 105th Congress, 1st sess. S. 769. <u>Thomas: Legislative Information on the Internet</u>. 10 Dec. 1997 <http://thomas.loc.gov>.

Report

United States. National Institutes of Health. <u>Changing Adolescent Smoking Prevalence</u>. Journal of the National Cancer Institute. Monograph 14. Washington: GPO, 2001.

Survey

United States. Dept. of Justice. <u>Criminal Victimization in the United States, 2003</u>. A National Crime Victimization Survey Report, NCJ-162126. Washington: GPO, 2003.

Hints

There are two federal Web sites:
- FedWorld Information Network (*http://www.fedworld.gov*)
- National Technical Information Service (*http://www.ntis.gov*)

Government publications are indexed in the *Monthly Catalog of United States Publications* and the *Public Affairs Information Service (PAIS) Bulletin*.

Information about foreign governments can be obtained from their embassies or from Web sites such as Wikipedia.org and Governments on the WWW (www.gksoft.com/govt), which supplies information free, or from yahoo.com, which requires a fee.

Nonprint Resources

Model	Explanation

Artwork

**Artist's last name, First name. <u>Title</u>.
[Date.] Institution that houses the
work or Owner, City.**

Begin with the artist's name. Then give the work's title. End with the location of the work.

☞ The date is optional. Place it after the title if you include it.

Painting

Maclise, Daniel. <u>The Play Scene in "Hamlet</u>."
1842. Tate Gallery, London.

CD-ROMs, Diskettes, or Magnetic Tape

CD-ROM Reference Work

<u>Merriam-Webster's Collegiate Dictionary</u>, 11th
ed. CD-ROM. Springfield, Mass: Merriam-
Webster, 2003.

Cite a reference published in CD-ROM or other such format as if it were a book; however, include *CD-ROM* (or *Diskette*, or *Magnetic Tape*) before the place of publication.

Databases

**Author's last name, First name. "Title."
<u>Original Source</u> date: [page(s)].
<u>Database</u>. Medium. Electronic
publication date.**

Databases allow you to search and retrieve articles from many sources. For example, InfoTrac has the full text of articles from more than 100 magazines available on CD-ROM. Some databases can be accessed online; costs vary.

When you cite an article from a database, begin with the author's name. After the article title, give the name of the original source (underlined) and the date of publication, followed by a colon. Then name the database, followed by a period. End with the electronic publication date.

Article from a Database

Caple, Jim. "Even at Age 64, Arnie Musters a
Loyal Army." <u>Knight Ridder/Tribune News
Service</u> 19 Aug. 1994: <u>InfoTrac SuperTOM</u>.
CD-ROM. Oct. 1997.

Films and Videos

Film

Gibson, Mel, perf. <u>Hamlet</u>. Dir. Franco Zefferelli.
Warner, 1990.

Matheson, Richard, adapt. <u>Dracula</u>. By Bram
Stoker. Dir. Dan Curtis. Perf. Jack Palance.
MPI Home Video, 1974.

Citations for films, filmstrips, DVDs, or videotapes usually begin with the title. If you are discussing an individual's work, however, begin with that person's name, followed by the title of the work. Then name the director, followed by a period. List the distributor, followed by a comma, and the date of release.

Videos/DVDs

<u>The Man on the Train</u>. Dir. Patrice Leconte. DVD.
Paramount, 2003.

☞ Other relevant information, such as performers or writers and the original release date, may be given after you identify the director. If you are citing a filmstrip, DVD, or film, include the medium before the name of the distributor.

Interviews

Interview

Greenside, Mark. Personal interview. 8 Feb.
2005.

Give the name of the person you talked with. Write *Personal interview*, followed by a period. End with the date of the interview.

Performances

Live performances are cited much like films. Include the date and location of the performance.

Stage Performance

<u>Riverdance</u>. Dir. John McColgan. Fox Theater, Detroit, MI. 20 May 2005.

Sound Recordings

The first name you list should be the name of the person you want to emphasize. If you're discussing the music in *Oklahoma!*, you might want to begin with the composer. If your focus is on character development or theme, beginning with the lyricist would make sense.

☞ If the recording is a CD, you do not need to note the medium.

☞ You may find these abbreviations helpful.

    Cond.—conducted by
    LP—long-playing record
    Orch.—orchestra
    Perf.—performed by
    Rec.—recorded

Author or performer. ["Song" or "Scene."] <u>Title of recording</u>. Date of recording. [Additional performers or writers.] Type of medium. Manufacturer, year of release.

Song on CD

Byrne, David. "Little Apocalypse." <u>Growing Backwards</u>. Nonesuch, 2004.

Play on Audiocassette

Shakespeare, William. <u>Hamlet</u>. Rec. Jan. 1992. Perf. Kenneth Branaugh and Renaissance Shakespeare Company. Audiocassettes. Bantam, 1992.

Opera on Long-Playing Record

Verdi, Guiseppe, composer. <u>Macbeth</u>. Lyrics by Francesco Maria Piave after William Shakespeare. LP. RCA Victor, 1959.

Speeches

Give the speaker's name (last name first). Give the title of the speech (with no quotation marks), the city where the speech was given, and the date. Use a period after each item.

Speech

Clinton, Bill. Inaugural Address. Washington, D.C. 20 Jan. 1997.

Television or Radio Programs

If a program aired in several episodes, first give the title of the episode in quotation marks. Then give the program title, underlined. If the program is part of a series, name the series. Then identify the network, the call letters and city of the local station on which the program aired, and the broadcast date.

☞ If you are discussing the work of a particular person, begin the entry with that person's name. For example, in a paper about Orson Welles, you might cite *The War of the Worlds* broadcast as follows.

    Welles, Orson, dir. <u>The War of the Worlds</u>. By H.G. Wells. Mercury Theatre on the Air. CBS Radio. WCBS, New York: 30 Oct. 1938.

Television Broadcast

"The New Asylums" <u>Frontline</u>. PBS. WGBH, Boston. 10 May 2005.

Television Series

<u>Middlemarch</u>. By George Eliot. Dir. Anthony Pope. 6 episodes. Masterpiece Theatre. PBS. WGBH, Boston. 10 Apr.–15 May 1994.

Radio Broadcast

<u>The War of the Worlds</u>. By H.G. Wells. Mercury Theatre on the Air. CBS Radio. WCBS, New York. 30 Oct. 1938.

Online Sources

Model   *Explanation*

Author's last name, First name. "Title."
Date site was visited. <Site
address/URL>.

E-mail Messages

Ross, Nathan. "Reply to Butler Act query."
E-mail to the author. 8 Jan. 2004.

Zabnov, Jan. E-mail to Sports and Academics
Committee, State High School Athletic
Association, Des Moines, IA. 2 Feb. 2005.

Online Interview

Shostak, Seth. Interview. 2 Dec. 2004.
    21 Apr. 2005. SpaceChat.
    <http://www.bbc.co.uk/science/space/
    spacechat/livechat/seth_shostak.shtml>.

Online Posting

Slater, Sara. Online posting. 14 Jan. 2005. Ask an
    Astronomer at Cornell University. 5 Dec. 2005
    http://curious.astro.cornell.edu/question.
    php?number=467>.

Hints

URL means online address. The letters stand
for Uniform Resource Locator.

Many online sources provide suggestions
about how to cite their information. You may
need to adapt the format to follow MLA style.

Internet Sources

When citing Internet sources, follow these general rules. Give the author's name, followed by a period. If no author is given, begin with the title in quotation marks, followed by a period. Give the date you visited the site, followed by a period. Give the site address—the URL—in angle brackets, followed by a period.

☞ Citations of online publications usually include information about the original printed source, which may be easier for some of your readers to find.

E-mail and Postings

To cite e-mail messages and online postings, give the author's name, followed by a period. Give the title of the e-mail or posting (if any), in quotation marks. Write a description of the communication, such as *Online posting*, followed by a period. Give the date of the e-mail or posting, followed by a period. Give the name of the forum (if any), followed by a period. End with the date of access and the URL enclosed in angle brackets, followed by a period.

☞ References to e-mail should include a description of the document that identifies the recipient. When you cite personal e-mail, you may use the phrase *E-mail to the author* instead of the actual e-mail address.

☞ You should always try to give the exact URL of any document you use. Some URLs are so long and cumbersome, however, that you may prefer to give the URL of the site's search page. The reader can use this URL to locate the information by keying in other information in the citation, such as the title or author's name.

Author's last name, First name. "Article
Title." Name of electronic journal
volume or issue number. (Year of
publication). Date of access <URL>.

Mitler, Merrill M., et al. "The Sleep of Long-Haul
    Truck Drivers." The New England Journal of
    Medicine On-Line 337.11 (1997). 17 Sept.
    1997 <http://www.nejm.org/public/
    1997/0337/0011/0755/1.htm>.

Electronic Journals

Ejournals, or electronic journals, are academic journals that are published online. Some may also appear in print.

Begin with the author's name and the article title in quotation marks. Give the name of the journal (underlined), followed by the volume number, the issue number, and a period. Give the date of publication in parentheses, followed by a colon. Give the number of pages, paragraphs, or other sections in the article. Then give the date on which you visited the site, followed by the electronic address in angle brackets. End with a period.

☞ If the article has numbered paragraphs, put a colon after the date of publication and give the number of paragraphs; for example, (2005): *5 pars.*

Explanation

Model

Online Newspapers and Magazines

Many periodicals now publish online versions that let subscribers keep up with breaking news. Even better, many have archives that you can search online.

Begin with the usual author and title information. Then give the name of the publication, which may be the same as the print newspaper or may include words like *Online*. Underline the title and place a period after it. Then give the original publication date, followed by a period. Next, give the date you accessed the text, followed by the electronic address in angle brackets.

☞ If section and page numbers are available, put a colon after the original publication date. Then give the section and page numbers, followed by a period.

> **Author's last name, First name.**
> **"Article Title." <u>Name of</u>**
> **<u>publication</u>. Original publication**
> **date. Date of access <URL>.**

Seidman, Carrie. "Jurassic Mac: Dentist Builds Business on Computer-Generated Dinosaur Models." <u>Albuquerque Journal</u>. 17 Sept. 1997. 2 June 2002 <http://www .abqjournal.com/scitech/1sci2-11.htm>.

Online Books and Articles

To cite a book or article found online, give the name of the author, compiler, translator, or editor. Give the title, underlined and followed by a period. Give the abbreviation *Comp.*, *Trans.*, or *Ed.*, if applicable, in parentheses. Give the original place of publication, followed by a colon. Give the publisher's name and the date. Identify the place where the text is located or archived, followed by a period. Give the date you accessed the text, followed by the electronic address in angle brackets. End with a period.

☞ If you are citing only part of an online book, insert the title or name of the part between the author's name and the book's title. If the title is an essay or a poem, put the title in quotation marks.

> **Author's last name, First name. <u>Text</u>**
> **<u>Title</u>. [Ed., Comp., or Trans. if**
> **applicable.] Original place of**
> **publication: Publisher, Date.**
> **Name of archive. Date of access**
> **<URL>.**

Sandburg, Carl. "Chicago." <u>Chicago Poems.</u> New York: Henry Holt and Company, 1916. <u>Bartleby.com: Great Books Online</u>. 21 Apr. 2005 <http://www.bartleby.com/165 /1.html>.

Web Sites

To cite a file you found on the Web, begin with the usual author and title information. If you know the date the document was created or updated, give that date, followed by a period. Then give the date you visited the site and the site's electronic address in angle brackets. Some browsers print the site address at the bottom of every sheet you print out from the site. You can also find the URL in a window at the top of your browser. Usually it begins *http://*. Follow the capitalization and punctuation in the site address exactly, and copy the entire address. End with a period.

☞ Citation style for referring to electronic sources is still evolving. Among the Web sites that provide updated style sheets are:

http://www.mla.org/main_stl.htm
http://www.bedfordstmartins.com/online/citex.html
http://owl.english.purdue.edu/handouts/research/rmla.html

> **Author's last name, First name.**
> **"Title." [<u>Title of complete work</u>.]**
> **[Date of the document, if**
> **available.] Date of your visit**
> **<Web site address>.**

Clark, Liesl. "Ice Mummies of the Inca." <u>Lost Worlds: The Sacrificial Ceremony</u>. 17 Sept. 1997. 14 Oct. 2000 <http://www.pbs.org/ wgbh/pages/nova/peru/worlds/sacrifice1 .html>.

- -

Rusche, Harry. "Hamlet's Crawl." 17 Sept. 1997. 8 Feb. 2000 <http://www.cc. emory.edu/ENGLISH/classes/Shakespeare _Illustrated/slither.html>.

3 Note Cards

If You Jot It, You've Got It

Note cards are used to record all information needed for the term paper. Note cards permit you to find information quickly and organize it easily.

A Typical Note Card

Write your information on index cards (usually 3" × 5"). Each card must have a short label to identify the subject of the information. The information follows in note form. You should also list the source—use the first word on your source card followed by the page numbers. (See Fig. 5.)

Hints

Some researchers like to keep their note cards in a large brown envelope. Others use recipe boxes. Finding some way to keep your note cards together will simplify your life.

If you have created a web or other graphic organizer on your topic, you might try using items from your web as labels.

Reminders

- Put a label and source on every card.
- Record only small amounts of information on each card.
- Use a dash to mean *to* and a comma to mean *and* in the page reference. (For example, 71–72 or 18, 20.)
- Abbreviate page numbers when practical. (For example, 117–19, not 117–119.) However, do not shorten numbers under 100 (55–58).
- Don't copy sentences from books without using quotation marks.
- Don't continue information from one card to another.
- Don't write on the backs of cards.
- Don't number cards.

Children at risk

    Risks for blacks twice as high as risks for whites:
      premature birth
      low birth weight
      living in substandard housing

        Edelman 53

Book censorship
Anticensorship group formed in Gwinnet County, Georgia, to challenge a censorship group on its requests to remove <u>Deenie</u> and <u>Go Ask Alice</u> from elementary schools.

Result: School board decides books will stay in schools.

        Bates 17

Fig. 5. Typical note cards.

More than One Source by the Same Author

When using more than one book by the same author, the source notation on each card must include the last name of the author, a shortened version of the title, and the page numbers. (See Fig. 6.)

Direct Quotations

In those cases where a direct quotation from the book may be useful, follow Fig. 7.

On the next page, you'll find models of different types of note cards.

Reminders

- Use quotation marks where needed.
- Use quotations to support your ideas.
- Use ellipses (three dots) when words within a sentence are left out. If words are left out at the end of a sentence, use the ellipses plus a final period (four dots in all).
- Don't use long quotations.

Suffrage—England, early 1900s

Mrs. Pankhurst led militant group of women.

Mrs. Fawcett led group interested in persuading leaders to give women the vote.

Tuchman, <u>Proud Tower</u> 353

Fig. 6. Note card showing more than one source by same author.

Suffrage—England, early 1900s

"Put off again and again by Asquith's promises to carry through Enfranchisement, which he made to secure quiet and never kept, the feminists in the years after 1909 slashed pictures in the National Gallery and set fires in cricket pavillions. . . ."

Tuchman, <u>Proud Tower</u> 382

Fig. 7. Note card for direct quotation.

Hints

If you lose your note cards, you'll have to repeat hours of work.

When writing notes by hand, put your name and phone number with your note cards. You might want to give the school's number instead of your home phone number.

When taking notes on a computer, make sure that you save your work every ten or fifteen minutes. Also be sure to make a backup copy and keep it somewhere other than your hard drive.

<table>
<tr><td>

Labor unrest, 1880–1900

"Between 1881 and 1894 over 14,000 labour contests had been fought, whereas strikes and lockouts had been almost unknown in 1870."

<u>Hillquit's History of Socialism in the United States</u> (1903), qtd. in Holloway 212

</td><td>

A Book Quoting Another Source

When a book quotes directly from another source, identify the original source reference, write the words *qtd. in*, the author's last name from the book you are reading, and the page numbers.

</td></tr>
<tr><td>

Quality of films

"...the beauty of a shot...depends on whether or not it explains what it seeks to explain."

Michelangelo Antonioni, qtd. in Ferguson 76

</td><td>

A Book Quoting a Person

When a book quotes a person directly, write the person's full name, the words *qtd. in*, the author's last name from the book you are reading, and the page numbers.

</td></tr>
<tr><td>

Communications—morality

Sees no conflict of values.
Television merely functions as voice of society.

Carter, letter, 17 May 1989

Function of poetry

The poem communicates feeling as well as ideas.

Blackhurst, interview, 12 June 1997

</td><td>

Interviews and Correspondence Information

Sometimes you may obtain information directly from a person in a letter or an e-mail or during an interview. If you have more than one contact with the person, include some details to identify which encounter you are citing. You might note the type of correspondence and date.

</td></tr>
<tr><td>

Causes of accidents

Greatest danger to bicycle riders is assuming that auto drivers will see them. Called auto drivers' "blindness."

<u>Cycle Safety</u>

</td><td>

Media Sources

To identify note cards from media references, write the short form of the title.

</td></tr>
<tr><td>

Nation's first attack

After Nation closed saloons in her home town (Medicine Lodge), local drinkers went to Kiowa. On June 1, 1890, she used "stones, brickbats, full malt bottles, and one billiard ball as ammunition" to attack three saloons in Kiowa.

cnation.html
29 Sept. 1997

</td><td>

Online Sources

In addition to the usual author and title information, you'll need the name of the online source and the date you accessed it. (You may need to hunt for the author's name; if it's not at the beginning of the document, it's often at the bottom of the page or at the end of the document.)

</td></tr>
</table>

A Few Questions and Answers

How many note cards?

There is no correct number of note cards. The number of cards you use depends on the amount of information recorded on each card and the complexity of the subject.

How do I know when I'm done?

When you begin your research, most of the information you find will be new. As you continue, you'll probably find that some information is familiar. Eventually, you'll find that you already know most of the information in your newest sources. At that point, you can stop researching.

How do I know I can trust a source?

One way to judge a source is by its reputation. Some authors are recognized as experts in their field. You can skim biographical information that you find with a book or article to check the author's background and credentials. You can also see if the author is associated with any reliable institutions.

With books and articles, you can judge the quality of an author's research by checking the works cited. This will give you an idea of how many works the author consulted and whether these works are reliable and up-to-date.

You can also look for evidence of bias. Does the author give the complete story? Objective coverage of issues should reflect opposing viewpoints. Does the author benefit by taking a particular position?

Be especially careful of Internet sources. The facts in books and articles are often (but not always) checked by editors. Many Web sites, however, are not edited. See who sponsors the Web site and look for a mission statement that lets you know its intent. Be sure the source is objective.

Check that the site is updated periodically, and be sure it covers the topic thoroughly. Find out if the site has an e-mail address that encourages further inquiries, and don't be afraid to contact them.

False information spreads rapidly in cyberspace. In fact, there is a United States government site devoted to tracking down and exposing Internet hoaxes called hoaxbusters.ciac.org.

How should I handle contradictions between sources?

Something isn't true just because it's in print.

Sometimes the errors are simple typos; for example, a date might be given as 9999 instead of 1999.

Sometimes the problem is a lack of information. For example, different sources may list an author's birth date as 1701, 1702, or 170?. Keep looking; you may find a source that explains the discrepancies. If not, you can either say "born around 1701" or note that "scholars disagree about the exact date."

You may read eyewitness accounts that contradict each other. In that case, you might mention each point of view and then give your interpretation of what really happened.

Sometimes you may not be able to figure out which source is most reliable. You might handle the problem in a parenthetical note. This example is from the sample paper in Appendix 1.

> Wrote defense lawyer Arthur Garfield Hays, it was "not just an ordinary prayer, but an argumentative one, directed straight at the defense" (qtd. in Weinberg 176, but other sources indicate differently: de Camp 175–76).

4 The Outline

The Bare Bones

An outline will help organize the information you have gathered, reveal the parts of the body that need more note cards, and prevent unnecessary work on irrelevant subjects. Before you begin to organize your material, think about how you plan to focus on your subject. You may use any of the following methods to organize your paper:

- Analytical: Investigating and classifying a subject
- Persuasive: Taking a point of view and arguing your case
- Compare/Contrast: Relating one subject to another, similar one
- Descriptive: Giving examples and details about a subject

Which of these approaches you choose will influence how you organize your paper, and should be apparent in your outline. An outline contains each of the items below.

The Question: This question, the main idea of your paper, should come directly from the topic card.

The Title: Rewrite the question in title form. Capitalize the key words.

I. The Introduction: This section will set the scene by giving general background information and stating the problem or issue to be discussed. The written introduction will have at least two paragraphs, but probably no more than four.
   A. *Background information*
   B. *Question from the topic card*

II. The Body: This section should provide all the information needed to answer the question in IB.

The labels on your note cards will correspond to the main topics of your outline, which you will indicate with a capital letter. Under each main topic you may have subtopics, indicated by numerals, and supporting points, indicated by lower-case letters. If the note card labels don't match the outline labels, you must change something. Perhaps you can modify one set of labels so they correspond. You might have to delete a group of note cards because they are not relevant to your question, or you may need to do more research.

Each main topic represents one or more paragraphs in the complete report. Arrange the labels in the order in which they will appear in the final report.

The rules of outlining require that for every Roman numeral *I* there must be a numeral *II* and that an *A* must be accompanied by a *B*. In other words, your outline should contain no lone numbers or letters.

III. The Conclusion: This third section will summarize the important evidence presented in the body of the paper. The conclusion will be brief, probably two or three paragraphs long. The outline for this section can read as follows:
   A. *Summary of the most important points*
   B. *Concluding paragraph: answer to the question*

IV. The Works Cited: This section is not a concern at the outline stage of the work. The outline can state: IV. *Works Cited.*

Reminders

- Use one of the models for outlining as your guide.
- Make sure the labels on the note cards match the labels in Section II of the outline.
- Put the labels in Section II into logical order.
- Make sure that each label in Section II is relevant to the question or problem stated in the introduction.
- In a topic outline, use phrases, except for the question and the problem.
- In a sentence outline, use sentences throughout.

Hint

The number of labels in Section II of the outline—the body—usually ranges from 4 to 12 for a paper that is 1,000 to 2,500 words. You may have more than 12 labels, especially for a 2,500-word paper.

Types of Outlines

There are two common outline types: the topic outline and the sentence outline.

The topic outline uses only short phrases to cover the various points you will be making in your paper. The sentence outline uses complete sentences.

If you do not have many labels on your note cards, or your paper is short, your outline might be simpler than the examples that follow. You may not need to use subtopics or supporting points.

Topic Outline

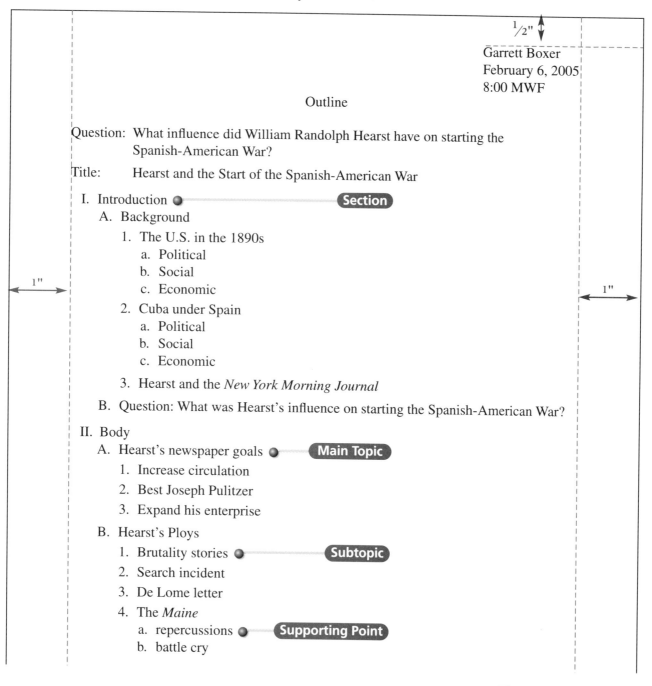

Garrett Boxer
February 6, 2005
8:00 MWF

Outline

Question: What influence did William Randolph Hearst have on starting the Spanish-American War?

Title: Hearst and the Start of the Spanish-American War

I.   Introduction ●━━━━━━━ **Section**
   A. Background
      1. The U.S. in the 1890s
         a. Political
         b. Social
         c. Economic
      2. Cuba under Spain
         a. Political
         b. Social
         c. Economic
      3. Hearst and the *New York Morning Journal*
   B. Question: What was Hearst's influence on starting the Spanish-American War?

II. Body
   A. Hearst's newspaper goals ●━ **Main Topic**
      1. Increase circulation
      2. Best Joseph Pulitzer
      3. Expand his enterprise
   B. Hearst's Ploys
      1. Brutality stories ●━ **Subtopic**
      2. Search incident
      3. De Lome letter
      4. The *Maine*
         a. repercussions ●━ **Supporting Point**
         b. battle cry

Fig. 8a. Topic Outline.
(Size of page is reduced.)

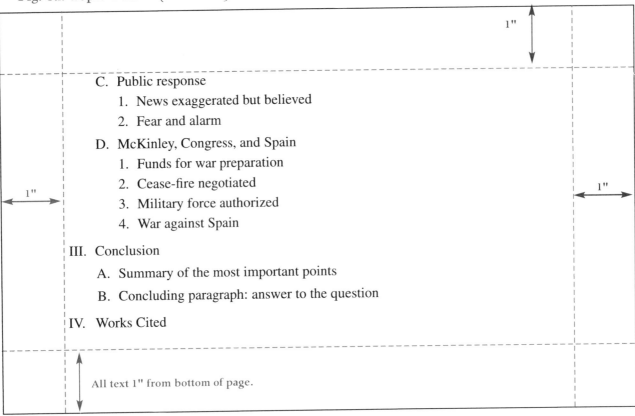

C. Public response
1. News exaggerated but believed
2. Fear and alarm

D. McKinley, Congress, and Spain
1. Funds for war preparation
2. Cease-fire negotiated
3. Military force authorized
4. War against Spain

III. Conclusion
A. Summary of the most important points
B. Concluding paragraph: answer to the question

IV. Works Cited

1"

1"

All text 1" from bottom of page.

Sentence Outline

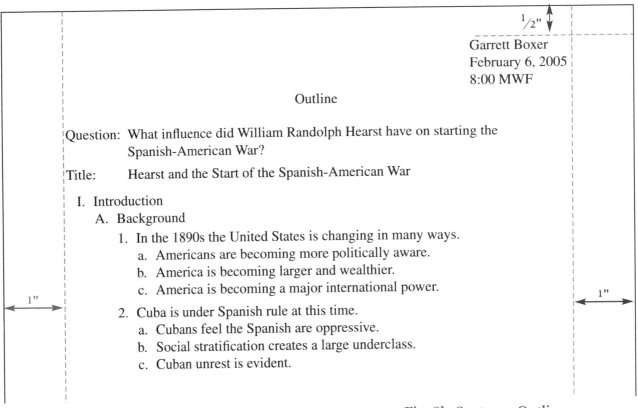

1/2"

Garrett Boxer
February 6, 2005
8:00 MWF

Outline

Question: What influence did William Randolph Hearst have on starting the Spanish-American War?

Title: Hearst and the Start of the Spanish-American War

I. Introduction
A. Background
1. In the 1890s the United States is changing in many ways.
a. Americans are becoming more politically aware.
b. America is becoming larger and wealthier.
c. America is becoming a major international power.
2. Cuba is under Spanish rule at this time.
a. Cubans feel the Spanish are oppressive.
b. Social stratification creates a large underclass.
c. Cuban unrest is evident.

1"

1"

Fig. 8b. Sentence Outline.
(Size of page is reduced.)

Fig. 8b. Sentence Outline (continued).

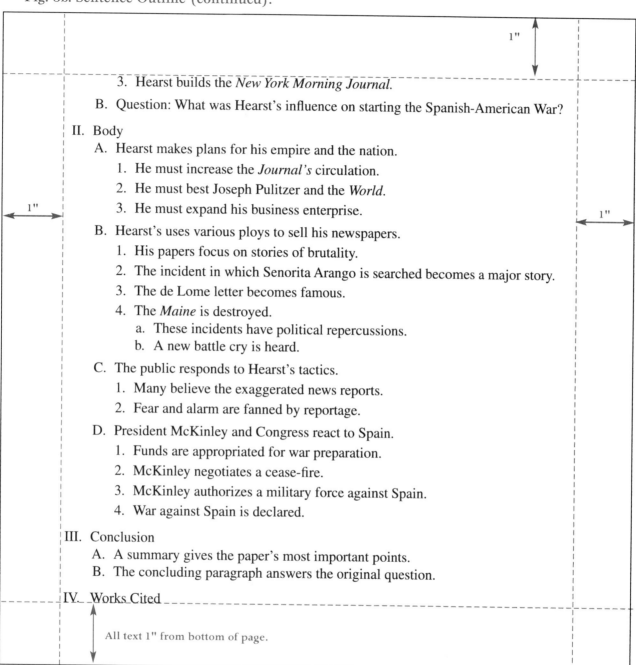

1"

      3. Hearst builds the *New York Morning Journal.*

   B. Question: What was Hearst's influence on starting the Spanish-American War?

II. Body

   A. Hearst makes plans for his empire and the nation.

      1. He must increase the *Journal's* circulation.

      2. He must best Joseph Pulitzer and the *World.*

      3. He must expand his business enterprise.

   B. Hearst's uses various ploys to sell his newspapers.

      1. His papers focus on stories of brutality.

      2. The incident in which Senorita Arango is searched becomes a major story.

      3. The de Lome letter becomes famous.

      4. The *Maine* is destroyed.

         a. These incidents have political repercussions.

         b. A new battle cry is heard.

   C. The public responds to Hearst's tactics.

      1. Many believe the exaggerated news reports.

      2. Fear and alarm are fanned by reportage.

   D. President McKinley and Congress react to Spain.

      1. Funds are appropriated for war preparation.

      2. McKinley negotiates a cease-fire.

      3. McKinley authorizes a military force against Spain.

      4. War against Spain is declared.

III. Conclusion

   A. A summary gives the paper's most important points.

   B. The concluding paragraph answers the original question.

IV. Works Cited

All text 1" from bottom of page.

5 The Rough Draft

Preparing to Write

Before you begin your rough draft, organize your workspace to make your information accessible. You will need all your note cards, the outline, and writing paper or a computer.

The rough draft brings your previous work together into one paper for the first time.

The writing process involves stages. A rough draft is not expected to be perfect. You will probably have to rewrite a good portion of it to create an excellent paper.

Arrange your note cards so that those with the same label are all together. All cards with a label that corresponds with Section II-A of your outline are in one stack. Next come all the cards that match Section II-B, then Section II-C, and so on.

If you write your draft by hand, use only one side of the paper, leaving a space between each line. If you are using a computer, double-space your draft.

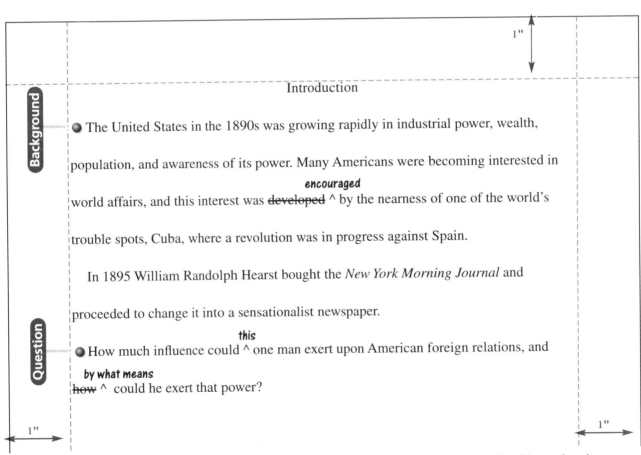

Fig. 9. Rough draft of introduction.
(Size of page is reduced.)

Writing the Main Idea and Introduction

Write a brief, general introduction to provide the background for your topic. This should be one or two paragraphs long, double-spaced. Usually, neither note cards nor acknowledgments are needed for the introduction. (See Fig. 9 on page 26.) Then, write the question, main idea, or thesis, of your paper. Because you now have more knowledge about your topic, you may wish to change a question to a statement.

Writing the Body

Take the cards labeled for topic II-A and spread them out in front of you. Read them and arrange them in logical order.

Now use the information from the cards in group II-A to write the first paragraph or two of the body. Remember to leave a space between lines. You may want to make changes or additions later. (See Fig. 10.)

When important information is used from a note card, you must document the source immediately after the cited material. This information comes from your note cards. (See Fig. 10.) Remember, you must document every quotation, important fact, or group of facts you include in your paper. In this way you give credit for information gained from someone else's work.

There is one exception to this principle: If you use your own words, you need not document *common knowledge*—well-known information found in more than one source.

Note: This example contains errors that will be shown corrected in Fig. 15, Chapter 6.

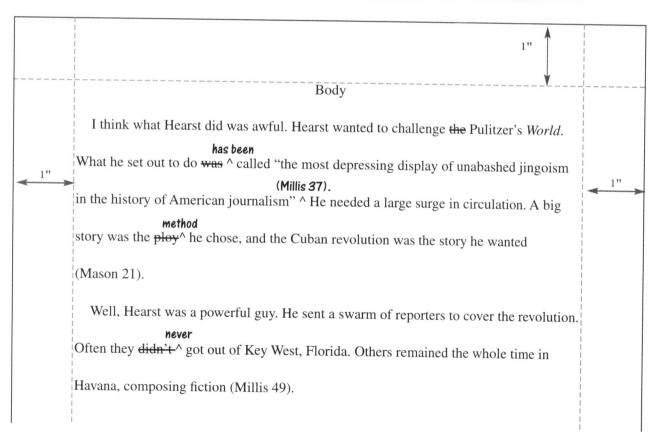

Fig. 10. Rough draft of body.
(Size of page is reduced.)

When all the facts in the paragraph come from the same source, documentation at the end of the paragraph is all that is needed. Occasionally, documentation may be needed at the end of each sentence in a paragraph. Sometimes two or more sources may be needed to document different facts in a single sentence.

Documentation is placed at the end of quotations, even if the quoted material is in the middle of the sentence.

Sometimes two books give similar information. If the facts are not common knowledge, or if they are debatable, mention both sources and separate them with a semicolon.

 The sample term papers in Appendix 1 show how documentation is used within a paper.

After you use a card, turn it over and place it in a separate stack out of your way. If a card is not used but still holds useful information, give it a new label and put the card in one of the stacks to follow. If a card has information that seems to have no immediate use, put it face up in a stack where it can be located later if needed.

When all the cards from the first group are used, spread out the cards labeled for the next topic. Write the next paragraph or paragraphs using these cards. Then go on to the remaining topic groups until all the appropriate cards have been used.

Long Quotations

For long quotations (more than four typed lines or more than 40 words handwritten), use block formatting. Indent the whole quotation ten typed spaces from the left margin (1 inch if your paper is handwritten).

If your long quotation is two or more paragraphs, indent the first line of each paragraph an additional three typewritten spaces (about $\frac{1}{4}$ inch handwritten). If you quote only part of the first paragraph, however, the first line of this partial paragraph is not indented an extra three spaces. You would still indent the first line of each subsequent paragraph.

Block quotations do not need quotation marks.

Be sure to place the documentation at the end of the quotation. (See Fig. 11.)

Identifying Illustrations

Maps, photographs, and other illustrations should be placed in the body of your paper. All illustrations should help readers understand your topic; they should never be mere decoration. For example, a map of Gettysburg might clarify your description of the battle that was fought there. If you use illustrations, place them as close as possible to the part of your paper they illustrate. (See page 63.)

Give each illustration a label, such as *Fig. 1, 2, 3,* and number them consecutively throughout your paper. Then give a brief description of the illustration: *Fig. 2. Shakespeare's stage adapted from DeWitt's drawing of the Swan Theatre (1596).* Captions are usually placed below the illustrations to which they refer.

Upon arrival at Auschwitz, families were torn apart:
An SS noncommissioned officer came to meet us, a truncheon in his hand. He gave the order:
"Men to the left! Women to the right!"
Eight words spoken . . . without emotion. Eight short, simple words. Yet that was the moment when I parted from my mother.
(Wiesel 27)

Fig. 11. Long quotation.

Identifying Tables

Numerical information is often presented in tables that arrange data in columns with rules and titles. For example, one way to show patterns of immigration would be in a graph or statistical table. (See Fig. 12.)

Tables should be given a label, such as *Table 1*. They should also have a title, placed one line below the label. (See Fig. 12.)

Crediting Illustrations and Tables

Refer the reader to an illustration or table when you first mention the idea it illustrates. You can write *(See Fig. 1.)* or *In Table 2*, etc. If the graphic doesn't fit on the page where it is mentioned, place it at the top of the next page.

Credit the source of all graphics. The source information is the same as on your note cards. (See Chapter 2.) The form is changed, however, as shown in the examples that follow.

For illustrations, place source information after the description. Begin with *from*. Then give the artist's first and last names, if known.

For tables, write *Source:* and the source information below the table. (See Fig. 12.)

What comes next depends on what type of source you are citing.

For books, add the author or editor's name, followed by a comma. Then give the title of the book, underlined. Follow this with the city of publication and a colon, the publisher, and the date in parentheses. Then give the page number.

Fig. 2. Map of Manhattan in 1664 from Carter Smith, ed., <u>Battles in America: A Sourcebook on Colonial America</u> (Brookfield: Millbrook Press, 1991) 41.

For magazines, again start with the description and *from* followed by the title in quotes, and the name of the magazine underlined. Follow with the date of publication, a colon, and the page number or numbers.

Fig. 3. Comparison of musicians' and nonmusicians' brains adapted from "Music of the Hemispheres," <u>Discover</u> Mar. 1994: 15.

For Web sites, include the underlined site name, any sponsoring organization, the date of access, and the site address in angle brackets.

Fig. 4. Satellite image of Ubar from <u>NASA Observatorium</u>, NASA, 1 Dec. 1997 <http://observe.ivv.nasa.gov/nasa/exhibits/ubar/ubar_3.html>.

Table 1

Patterns of Chinese Immigration per Decade

1850	4,825	1920	61,639
1860	34,933	1930	74,954
1870	63,199	1940	77,504
1880	105,465	1950	117,629
1882	132,300	1960	198,958
1890	107,488	1970	435,062
1900	89,863	1980	812,178
1910	71,531	1990	1,645,000

Source: <u>Dragonwings Latitudes</u> (Logan: Perfection Learning, 1995) 18.

Fig. 12. A table in a research paper.

Writing the Conclusion

Write one or two paragraphs that summarize the important points presented in the body of the paper. Do not introduce any new information in the conclusion.

Then write a short paragraph that answers the question.

The conclusion is the only part of the paper where your own judgment can be expressed—but not in first-person form. This judgment should be based on the information presented in the paper.

Note cards and documentation are not needed for the conclusion unless you use a quotation (Fig. 13).

A Comment About Length and Numbers

Your teacher may ask you to write a paper that includes a specific number of words or pages. (Handwritten pages usually have 200–250 words per page. Typed pages average 500 words per page.) Looking at other papers that are about the right length will help you gauge how much you can cover within those limits.

If you are given no specific requirements, individual judgment about each paper is the most important factor in determining length. No arbitrary counting of words, note cards, or acknowledgments will produce a good paper. An excessively long paper is as undesirable as one that is so skimpy it does not deal with the subject adequately.

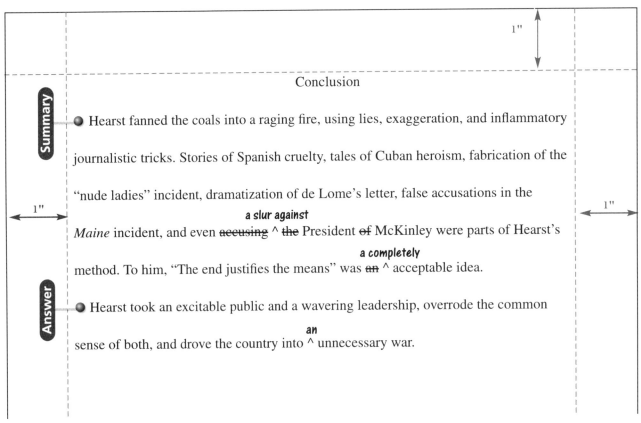

Fig. 13. Rough draft of conclusion.
(Size of page is reduced.)

More Questions and Answers

How much documentation is needed?

While there is no fixed number, a 1,000-word paper would almost certainly require ten or more citations. A 2,500-word paper would probably include more than 20 references.

May all documentation refer to one book?

No! Even if other books give the same information, refer to at least three different sources in your paper.

Are quotations the only words that need documentation?

No! All significant information, as well as quotations, must be acknowledged.

Is documentation required for every note card used?

No. Sometimes one acknowledgment refers to the information from several cards, or from one card, or from only part of one card. Documentation refers to information, not to note cards.

Should I underline or use italics when referring to book titles, the names of ships or trains, and so on?

If you write your term papers with a computer, you can easily use italics to indicate book titles and the names of ships or trains. This is the preferred form. However, you should check with your teacher. He or she may prefer that you underline such references.

Can information be used that is given by another person?

Yes, provided the person is a knowledgeable source. Refer to the person in an acknowledgment, as shown in Fig. 14 below.

What happens to someone caught plagiarizing?

The penalties for plagiarism—copying someone else's work without acknowledging it—vary. Some teachers give an F for the paper or for the entire course. At some colleges, students are expelled. Professionals who copy other people's work lose their credibility and may also lose their jobs. For more on plagiarism, see pages 46–48.

May a first- or second-person form be used?

In formal papers, *I, me, you,* or *one* (in the sense of *you*) should not be used anywhere, except in a quotation. Avoid statements like "I think that figure skating is a very demanding sport." Instead, state your opinion by providing evidence to prove it. "Top figure skaters have extraordinary stamina . . . ."

> *is used only in very rare cases (Garfield interview), and this opinion is held by many in the scientific field. (Ross, letter, 20 May 2004).*

Fig. 14. Acknowledgments for interviews and correspondence.

6 Revisions

Smoothing the Rough Draft

Carefully checking and revising the rough draft will make writing the final draft relatively easy.

Make all the following revisions on the rough draft. Do not recopy the paper at this stage. Simply write in changes where needed. See Fig. 15, which shows a revised page.

1. Read the section titles. Change the heading **Body** to a title that indicates the kind of information the section contains. The headings **Introduction** and **Conclusion** should also be changed to suitable titles.

The example below comes from a paper about William Randolph Hearst and the Spanish-American War. The introduction is titled **America's Mood Before Hearst**. The body becomes **Hearst's Methods and Their Effects**. The conclusion is renamed **Hearst's Influence**.

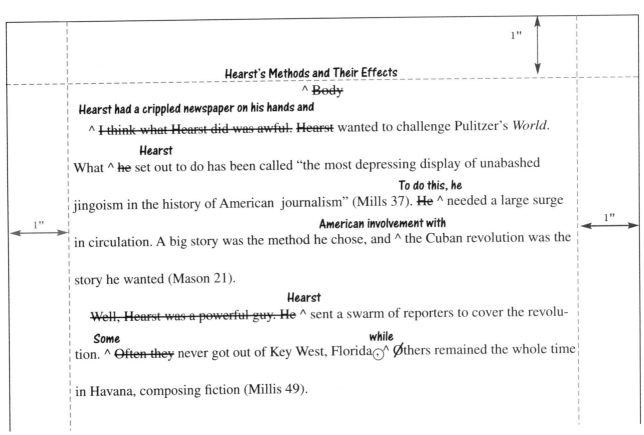

Fig. 15. Rough draft page revised.
(Size of page is reduced.)

2. Read the introduction to make sure all the information is background for the question the paper asks or the issue presented. The question or issue must be clearly stated. Every sentence should be relevant to this question or issue.

---

3. Read the body to make sure that everything in it pertains to the question or issue stated in the introduction. Cross out any irrelevant material. Make sure that no personal opinion is expressed in this section.

---

4. Read the conclusion to see that no new material is introduced. Make sure the important evidence is presented in a brief summary. A clearly stated answer must be given to the question asked or a solution offered to the issue posed in the introduction. The conclusion is the only section in which a personal opinion is permissible—but not in first-person form and not out of context.

---

5. Make sure you have labeled, numbered, and documented any maps, illustrations, or tables. (See Fig. 16.)

---

6. Read through the entire paper again to eliminate any first- or second-person forms such as I, me, you, or one. Cross out and revise any present-tense words that may have crept in where they are not proper. Make sure that each person's name is given in full the first time it is used (except in parenthetical documentation). The tone of the paper should be formal. Careful word choice is expected.

---

7. Read the paper once more to make sure every paragraph has a unity of its own. Change paragraph divisions, if necessary, to achieve unity. Eliminate irrelevant material.

---

8. Check the entire paper for spelling with a dictionary or spellchecker. Remember that spellcheckers won't catch errors such as using their instead of there.

---

9. Go through your paper again. This time examine the punctuation. Be careful to correct run-ons and sentence fragments.

---

10. Finally, ask a friend or parent to read the paper and offer suggestions. He or she may see things that are invisible to you. This is not a suggestion that your reader should rewrite the paper or proof it in detail. This person, however, should be able to give a general evaluation of your approach and to provide suggestions.

The OVERSHADOWING CURSE

THE LEGALIZED SALOON
HAS SHE A FAIR CHANCE?

"Our religion demands that every child should have a fair chance for citizenship in the coming Kingdom. Our patriotism demands a saloonless country and a stainless flag."--P. A. Baker, General Superintendent Anti-Saloon League of America.

Fig. 1. Antisaloon poster from The Library of Congress.

Fig. 16. Illustration and caption.

7 Documentation

Acknowledging Sources

Before you write the final draft, check the documentation.

Read through your rough draft again and check to make sure that all words and ideas that are not your own are documented. If you find quotations or ideas that need to be documented, add parentheses and an acknowledgment, which can be found in your note cards.

Documentation in your paper comes from your note cards. Usually, these are already in the proper form. This chapter shows you how to be sure all documentation is correct. It also reviews documentation of some common and not-so-common types of sources.

If you do not find an example of documentation to fit a particular type of source in this chapter, check pages 6-7 or ask your teacher for further instruction.

Remember, all documentation must point to a source in the works cited at the end of the paper and also tell where in that source the words or ideas you used can be found.

Reminders

- Punctuate correctly following the models in Chapter 3.
- Put end-of-sentence punctuation after parenthetical references. The only exception is a long quotation. In that case, the punctuation is placed at the end of the quotation and before the parentheses.
- Use a dash between page numbers to indicate *to*.
- Use a comma between page numbers to indicate *and*.
- Don't use *p.* or *pp.* before page numbers.

Model

At the beginning of the novel, Chief of Police Clumly represents law and order, while the Sunlight Man represents "absolute, anarchistic freedom" (Cowart 63).

As J. Dover Wilson suggests, Hamlet must test the Ghost to see if the spirit comes from Heaven or Hell (53).

Explanation

Typical Documentation

The most common way to acknowledge a source is to cite the author's last name and page numbers inside parentheses following the quotation or idea in your paper.

If the author's name appears within the sentence or paragraph, then only the page number needs to be inside the parentheses.

Two or More Works by the Same Author

If using two or more works by the same author, distinguish one work from another in the body of your paper. Therefore, document the author's words or ideas by writing the author's last name, a comma, a shortened form of the title you are borrowing from, and the page number(s).

> Prime Minister Asquith promised women the vote several times but did not carry through with this promise. His chief aim was only to quiet the feminists (Tuchman, Proud Tower 353).

Authors with the Same Last Name

Sometimes you might use two or more sources by different authors with the same last name. To document one author's words or ideas, write in parentheses the author's first name or initial and last name, followed by the page number(s) from which you took the information.

> In his 1967 State of the Union address, when President Johnson appealed for civil rights, there was not a single handclap. However, his appeal to save the redwood trees received loud approval (John Griffin 176).

Multiple Authors

If using a source written by more than one author, document in one of these ways:

   If the work has two or three authors, write all the last names of the authors, followed by the page number(s) in parentheses. Be sure to write *and* before the last author's name. (Separate three authors' names with commas.)

   If the work has more than three authors, write the last name of the first author listed, followed by *et al.* (meaning "and others"), and the page number(s).

> should not be read as history. Even the playwrights caution against this (Lawrence, Smith, and Lee, preface).

> Job sharing may be an option for a professional couple who want to split a high-paying job. A couple sharing a low-paying job, however, could not survive (Swerdlow et al. 158).

Corporate Authors

For a corporate author, document by giving the corporate name or a shortened form.

   Many corporate authors have shortened names. For example, the United Nations Educational, Scientific, and Cultural Organization is known by its full name and by its short name, UNESCO. If you are using material from this organization, you would simply write UNESCO, followed by the page number(s) in parentheses.

> In Belize, the number of physicians increased from 1976 to 1978 (World Bank 2: 9).

Sacred Texts

If the title of the sacred text is mentioned, cite only the chapter and verse.

> The Old Testament prophet Jeremiah encouraged his people to "Execute justice in the morning, and deliver from the hand of the oppressor him who has been robbed...." (Jer. 21.12).

Model	Explanation
Since World War II, there have been at least fifteen major military conflicts worldwide (<u>Chronicle</u> 1292).	**Documenting by Title** A source for which you have no author should be cited by title. Use the title or a shortened form in parentheses.
Even at his death, James Joyce and his writing were maligned by critics. However, one voice of approval was heard from T.S. Eliot, who highly praised Joyce's story "The Dead" (Deming 757).	**Multiple-Volume Works** To document material from a multiple-volume work, include the volume number if you used facts from more than one volume in your paper. Give the author's name and the volume number, followed by a colon and the page number (Boswell 2: 450). If you used facts from only one volume, do not cite the volume number.
Beneatha warns Mama not to ask Asaigai "a whole lot of ignorant questions about Africans" (Hansberry 45; sc. 2).	**Literary Works** Literary works are often cited by chapter, stanza, act, scene, or line.
Following the Jameson Raid, Cecil Rhodes resigned as Prime Minister of the Cape Colony ("Rhodes").	**One-Page Articles** One-page articles, such as sections from encyclopedias, do not need page numbers.
Sophocles' character Oedipus killed his father along the road from Thebes to Eleusis and then climbed the hills of Cithaeron where he encountered a sphinx (<u>Gods and Men</u>).	**Media Sources** For nonprint media—filmstrips, DVDs, videocassettes, films, audiocassettes—document by author's last name (if author is known) and shortened title.
In a letter to Josephine Herbst, Katherine Porter wrote about the links that bind people: I believe we exist on a half dozen planes and inhabit all periods of time at once, by way of memory, racial experience, dreams that are another channel of memory. (qtd. in Unrue 29)	**Quotations from Another Book or Person** When using material that an author found in another book or obtained from another person, follow the quote, paraphrase, or idea with parentheses, the words *qtd. in*, the source you got the information from, and the page number(s).

Two or More Sources to Support the Text

Sometimes the same information is supported by two or more sources. If you wish to acknowledge all these sources, use one parenthetical reference that includes all sources. Separate each work with a semicolon.

They had to settle for a jury composed of six Baptists, four Methodists, and one Disciple of Christ. Only one juror did not attend church (Ragsdale 100; Settle 75).

Long Quotations

Place the final punctuation at the end of a long indented quotation. Then, in parentheses, give the source and page number(s).

In a letter to Josephine Herbst, Katherine Porter wrote about the links that bind people:

> I believe we exist on a half dozen planes and inhabit all periods of time at once, by way of memory, racial experience, dreams that are another channel of memory. (qtd. in Unrue 29)

References Cited in Text

If you refer to an author or work in a sentence, there is no need to repeat the author or work in the parentheses. In such cases, a reference to the page number(s) is enough.

Ray Ginger reported that two days later, all permits in Dayton were canceled for the duration of the trial (100).

Online and Electronic Sources

In most cases, a page number will not be available for online and electronic sources. If you know the author, give the author's name in parentheses. If paragraph numbers are given, include the paragraph number. Otherwise, refer to a key word in the title; choose a word from your source card.

"Before the age of eighteen, the average American teen will have witnessed eighteen thousand simulated murders on TV" (Fanning).

Shakespeare's Henry V was probably the first play performed at The Globe (Sohmer 17).

The cracks of the plaster are first filled with gluten and then fastened with brass clasps shaped like a T. ("Specimen of Pompeian Fresco Painting.")

Sorting Your Source Cards

When you've documented your draft, make sure you have a source card for each source you mentioned in parenthetical documentation. Alphabetize these source cards. (See Fig. 17.) Ignore the words *the*, *a*, and *an* when alphabetizing. (See The Revised English Bible below.)

Do not discard any source cards. You may still add information from these sources to the final draft.

Swerdlow, Amy, Renate Bridenthal, Joan Kelly, and Phyllis Vine. Household and Kin: Families in Flux. Old Westbury: Feminist; New York: McGraw, 1981.

Settle, Mary Lee. The Scopes Trial: The State of Tennessee v. John Thomas Scopes. New York: Watts, 1972.

The Revised English Bible with Apocrypha. London: Oxford UP, 2003.

Ragsdale, W.B. "I Remember Three Weeks in Dayton." American Heritage June 1975: 35+.

Fig. 17. Sample source cards in alphabetical order.

A Fine Finale

The final draft prepares the paper for presentation. There will be no new work at this point. You are merely setting up the paper in proper form.

The final draft is double-spaced. It may be handwritten or typed on a computer. In any case, the draft must be neat and easy to read. Use only one side of an $8\frac{1}{2}$" × 11" piece of paper.

Typewritten papers should have a 1-inch margin on all sides, except for the title page, which is centered on all lines. The first line of each new paragraph should be indented five typed spaces from the left margin. An entire long quotation should be indented ten typed spaces. (See additional spacing rules for quotations on page 28.)

Handwritten papers should align with the red-line margin on the left side of the paper. The right-hand margin should be as close to 1 inch as possible. Indent the first line of each paragraph about $\frac{1}{2}$ inch from the left margin, and indent long quotations about 1 inch. (See additional spacing rules for quotations on page 28.) Begin writing on the first full line of the page, and leave three or four lines blank at the bottom of every page.

First or Title Page

There are two widely used formats for the beginning of your paper. Your teacher will tell you which one to use.

If you use a modern condensed format such as suggested in *The MLA Handbook* begin your paper with your last name and the page number (1) in the upper right corner. Skip a line; then write

- your name
- your teacher's name
- the name of the course
- the day, month, and year (24 May 2005)

Skip another line and center the title of your paper. Use capital and lowercase letters. The introduction follows.

If you use a more traditional format, start with a title page. The title page will show the title, the word *by* (not capitalized), your name, the course title, class period, instructor's name, and the due date. Every line of a title page, typed or handwritten, is centered on the page. Capitalize the first letters of the first, last, and most important words in the title. Do not capitalize an article, preposition, or coordinating conjunction unless such a word is the first or last word in the title. Study the examples in

Appendix Item

Fig. 18 (on page 40) and Appendixes 1, 2, and 3.

Reminders

- Capitalize the first, last, and most important words in the title.
- Space the page correctly.
- Underline only things that are normally underlined, such as the title of a book.
- Don't put quotation marks around the title.

Hints

If you write your paper using a computer, save your work frequently. Also have a backup copy on your hard drive and on a disk for safety's sake.

Read your entire paper to catch any grammar or spelling problems. If you have a spellchecker, run it before you print your final draft. Be aware that spellcheckers don't catch homonyms—it won't alert you if you use *here* when you mean *hear*.

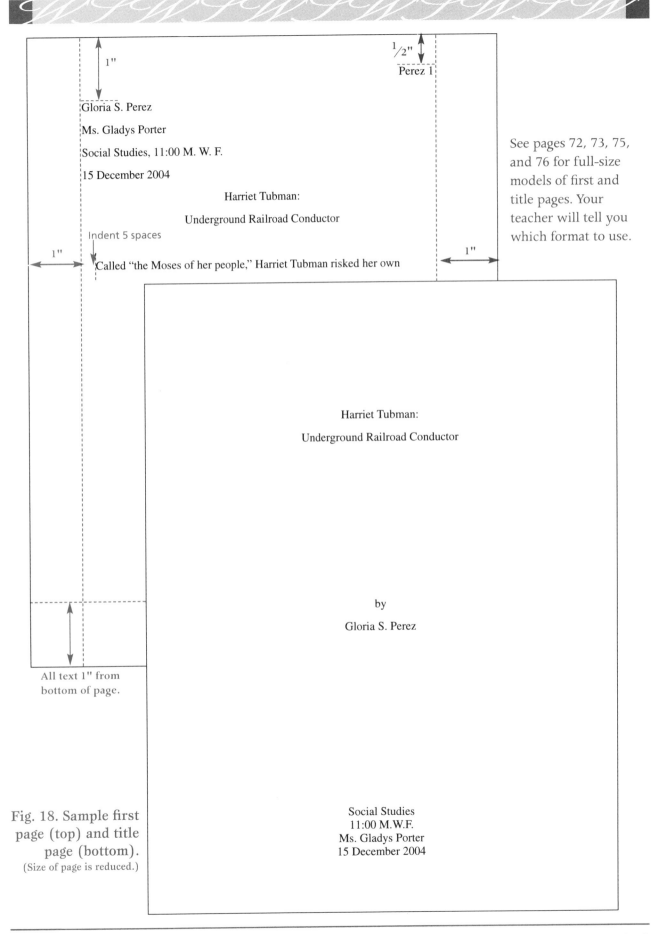

1"

1/2"

Perez 1

Gloria S. Perez

Ms. Gladys Porter

Social Studies, 11:00 M. W. F.

15 December 2004

Harriet Tubman:

Underground Railroad Conductor

Indent 5 spaces

1"

Called "the Moses of her people," Harriet Tubman risked her own

1"

See pages 72, 73, 75, and 76 for full-size models of first and title pages. Your teacher will tell you which format to use.

All text 1" from bottom of page.

Harriet Tubman:

Underground Railroad Conductor

by

Gloria S. Perez

Social Studies
11:00 M.W.F.
Ms. Gladys Porter
15 December 2004

Fig. 18. Sample first page (top) and title page (bottom).
(Size of page is reduced.)

Introduction, Body, and Conclusion

After you have centered the title of your paper, skip another line and write the section title for your introduction. Always center section titles. Then indent five spaces if typing or ½ inch if writing by hand. Begin to write the introduction by carefully copying your rough draft. Continue to double-space. Stop writing 1 inch from the bottom of the page if typing. If you are making a handwritten copy, leave three or four blank lines at the bottom. (See Appendixes 2 and 3.)

Then begin page two on a fresh sheet of paper. The text on the second and subsequent pages should begin 1 inch from the top for typewritten papers or on the first full line for handwritten ones.

The body follows the introduction and is handled in the same way. Skip one line after the introduction (unless you are beginning a new page). Then begin the body with its section title. Skip one line and copy the body from the rough draft. Do the same for the conclusion. (See Fig. 19.)

Page Numbers

Number all pages right through to the end of the works cited section.

The page number should be placed in the upper right corner, ½ inch from the top of each page. Write or type your last name and then the page number on every page except the title page. The placement of numbers is shown on the sample pages in Appendixes 2 and 3.

Reminders

- Stay within the margins.
- Start all the pages on the same line, whether they have section titles or not.
- Indent long quotations ten spaces or 1" from the left margin. Use no quotation marks.
- Double-space throughout the text.
- When typing, leave the right margin unjustified or uneven for readability.
- Leave 1" at the bottom of typewritten papers, or 3 to 4 blank lines at the bottom of handwritten papers.

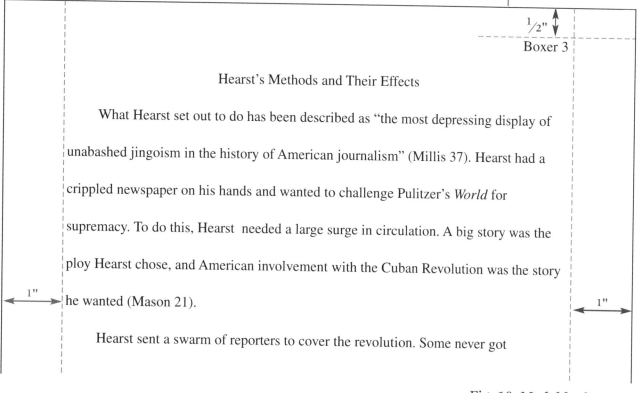

½"

Boxer 3

Hearst's Methods and Their Effects

What Hearst set out to do has been described as "the most depressing display of unabashed jingoism in the history of American journalism" (Millis 37). Hearst had a crippled newspaper on his hands and wanted to challenge Pulitzer's *World* for supremacy. To do this, Hearst needed a large surge in circulation. A big story was the ploy Hearst chose, and American involvement with the Cuban Revolution was the story he wanted (Mason 21).

Hearst sent a swarm of reporters to cover the revolution. Some never got

1"   1"

Fig. 19. Model body page.
(Size of page is reduced.)

9 The Works Cited

Once Over Rightly

The works cited is a record of all the printed materials and media sources used in writing your paper.

Write or type *Works Cited* 1 inch from the top of a typewritten page or on the first full line of the handwritten page. Leave one blank line after the title. Then, leaving a 1-inch margin at the left, copy the source cards onto your paper. Double-space all information. Entries should be in alphabetical order according to the author's last name. Use the reverse indentation system. The author's name should extend to the left margin, and all other lines should be indented five typed spaces or approximately $\frac{1}{2}$ inch handwritten. Stay within the margins.

When no author is listed, alphabetize the work according to the first word of the title. If the first word in the title is *a, an* or *the*, alphabetize by the second word.

If two works by the same author are listed, insert three hyphens and a period (---.) in place of the author's name at the start of the second and later references.

Check the form of each entry carefully. Apply the rules explained in Chapter 2.

Study the model list of works cited. (See Fig. 20, pages 43-44, **Appendix Item** and the sample term papers in Appendix 1.) Make sure your list corresponds with the samples.

Reminders

- Use the reverse indentation system.
- Put the author's last name before the first.
- Write any co-authors' names first name first. (Follow the Evans and Boyte example on page 43.)
- Underline book, magazine, newspaper, film, and filmstrip titles. Other style manuals may suggest that you italicize these.
- Put quotation marks around titles of articles from magazines, newspapers, and anthologies.
- Abbreviate the names of the publishers.
- Punctuate correctly.
- Remember the period at the end of each entry.
- Keep all the margins clean.

Works Cited Models

Check the author references in Fig. 20 for each of the following examples.

Books: Solzhenitsyn and Wiesel

Book with two authors: Evans

Magazine article: Frazier

Newspaper article: Swoboda

Article from a database: Caple

Anthology articles: Montaigne and Toelken

Media source: Monuments of Ancient Greece

Editor and complete anthology: Swann

Author plus editor: Faulkner

Pamphlet and missing information: "Drugs and Our Children"

Two or more works by the same author: Solzhenitsyn

Web site: McCabe and Cusac

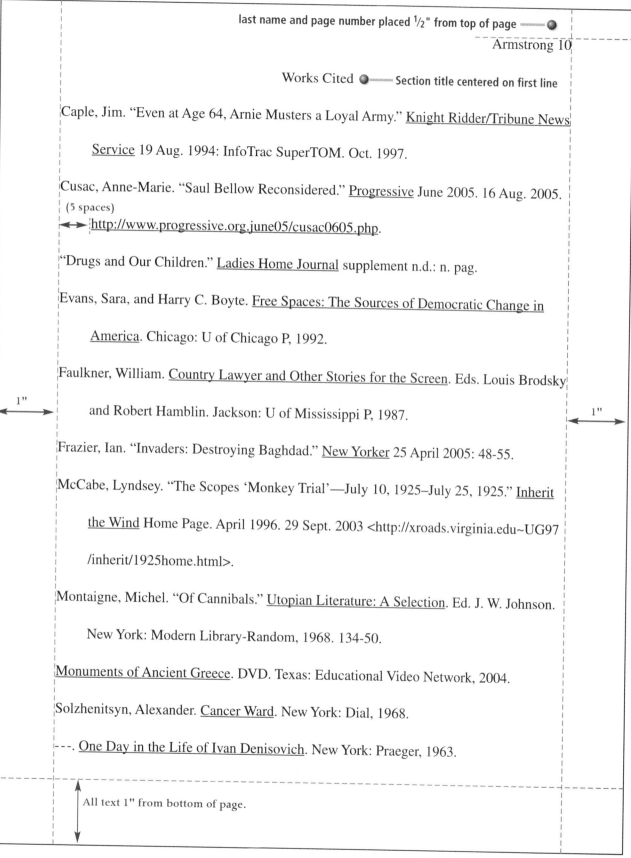

last name and page number placed ½" from top of page ●

Armstrong 10

Works Cited ● —— Section title centered on first line

Caple, Jim. "Even at Age 64, Arnie Musters a Loyal Army." <u>Knight Ridder/Tribune News</u>

<u>Service</u> 19 Aug. 1994: InfoTrac SuperTOM. Oct. 1997.

Cusac, Anne-Marie. "Saul Bellow Reconsidered." <u>Progressive</u> June 2005. 16 Aug. 2005.

(5 spaces)

◄——► <u>http://www.progressive.org.june05/cusac0605.php</u>.

"Drugs and Our Children." <u>Ladies Home Journal</u> supplement n.d.: n. pag.

Evans, Sara, and Harry C. Boyte. <u>Free Spaces: The Sources of Democratic Change in</u>

<u>America</u>. Chicago: U of Chicago P, 1992.

Faulkner, William. <u>Country Lawyer and Other Stories for the Screen</u>. Eds. Louis Brodsky

and Robert Hamblin. Jackson: U of Mississippi P, 1987.

Frazier, Ian. "Invaders: Destroying Baghdad." <u>New Yorker</u> 25 April 2005: 48-55.

McCabe, Lyndsey. "The Scopes 'Monkey Trial'—July 10, 1925–July 25, 1925." <u>Inherit</u>

<u>the Wind</u> Home Page. April 1996. 29 Sept. 2003 <http://xroads.virginia.edu~UG97

/inherit/1925home.html>.

Montaigne, Michel. "Of Cannibals." <u>Utopian Literature: A Selection</u>. Ed. J. W. Johnson.

New York: Modern Library-Random, 1968. 134-50.

<u>Monuments of Ancient Greece</u>. DVD. Texas: Educational Video Network, 2004.

Solzhenitsyn, Alexander. <u>Cancer Ward</u>. New York: Dial, 1968.

---. <u>One Day in the Life of Ivan Denisovich</u>. New York: Praeger, 1963.

All text 1" from bottom of page.

1"   1"

Fig. 20. Model works cited page.

(Size of page is reduced.)

Fig. 20. Model works cited (continued).

Swann, Brian, and Arnold Krupat, eds. <u>Recovering the Word: Essays on Native American Literature</u>. Berkeley: U of California P, 1987.

Swoboda, Frank. "Panel Votes to Raise Minimum Wage." <u>The Washington Post</u> 4 Mar. 1988: A15.

Toelken, Barre. "Life and Death in the Navajo Coyote Tales." <u>Recovering the Word: Essays on Native American Literature</u>. Eds. Brian Swann and Arnold Krupat. Berkeley: U of California P, 1987. 388-401.

Wiesel, Elie. <u>Night</u>. Trans. Stella Rodway. Toronto: Bantam, 1982.

1"

1"

All text 1" from bottom of page.

Putting It All Together

Careful assembly assures that your work will be presented in the most effective way.

Final Checklist

Look through the paper carefully, checking the following items:

- ● First or title page is in correct format
- ● All writing is within margins
- ● Page numbers are placed at top right corner, $\frac{1}{2}$" from top (not in right margin)
- ● Section titles are in correct format
- ● Text is double-spaced
- ● All pages start on the same line
- ● Works cited page is properly spaced and indented

Assembly

Put the finished paper in a simple folder that holds the pages securely. Pages should lie flat when the folder is opened.

Include in the folder the title page (if used), the paper itself, and the list of works cited.

A Last Word

Your term paper should at last be in good form. The hours you spent researching and writing have greater impact because your presentation is professional and well planned.

This ability to effectively prepare written material is an important skill. In the future—perhaps in another class, perhaps on the job—you may be asked to work on a similar project. Whether it is another term paper, a monthly report, an expense account, or a job proposal, you will know how to organize and convey your message.

After all, that's what "writing in style" means: presenting information in the correct form for your audience. By learning the rules in this guide, you've developed the skills for effective communication.

Reminders

- If illustrations are essential, place them near the material they illustrate.
- Don't include a contents page, outline, rough draft, or index cards unless your teacher requests them.
- Don't add a circle, period, parentheses, quotation marks, *p.*, or *pp.* to the page number.
- Don't crowd the page number against the edge of the page.
- Don't include blank pages.
- Don't include decorations or designs.

11 Using Sources Honestly

Plagiarism

Using someone's writing without attributing that writing to the person is plagiarism. When you plagiarize, you present someone else's ideas, language, or impressions as your own. You are, in effect, stealing. When writing a research report or term paper, you must be careful to always give credit to authors.

The word *plagiarism* comes from a Latin word meaning "kidnapper." The charge of plagiarism may not be on a par with kidnapping, but it is a very serious offense. Plagiarists are seen as devoid of their own intellectual integrity. They are people who snatch the ideas of others instead of working to express their own thoughts. To steer clear of any hint of plagiarism always check your paper for acknowledgments.

The best way to avoid plagiarism is to use your own words. When you use your own words to express someone else's ideas you are *paraphrasing*. You must credit the source of your paraphrased text because the idea did not originate with you. Use quotation marks to indicate text you are picking up from another's writing. This way you acknowledge that you are using the author's exact words. Be sure you have quoted, documented, or otherwise attributed any ideas or words that did not come directly from your brain.

It has been estimated that 58 percent of high school students have committed "cut and paste" plagiarism by presenting text taken directly from the Internet as their own. That's an alarmingly high percentage. It is quite possible that some of these students are not aware that copying material without citing it is unlawful and unethical. It is also possible that some of these students are trying to "get away with something." Don't kid yourself. Stealing an author's words and ideas is no different than stealing a car or a wallet. And don't think your teacher will be fooled. Most teachers say they can easily tell when a student's writing is lifted directly from an unnamed source. The following information should help you avoid even inadvertent plagiarism.

Example of Plagiarism #1: Using Another's Words

Look at the passage below from the book *Reading the World: Contemporary Literature from Around the Globe*. Take a few quick notes about the passage. Then write the information in your own words.

Original Passage

As the Emperor of China, Aisin-Gioro P'u Yi had for a brief time exceptional power and wealth. In 1908, at age three, P'u Yi assumed his title, but the Republican Revolution four years later forced him to relinquish his throne.

If your writing is anything like the passage below, you are guilty of plagiarism because you have used ideas without acknowledgement, even though you changed it a good deal.

Plagiarized Passage

Aisin-Gioro P'u Yi became Emperor of China in 1908, at the age of three. Four years later he was removed from his throne by the Republican Revolution.

Be sure to write the information in your own words and cite the source that gave you the information, as in the example below.

Properly Cited Passage

Aisin-Gioro P'u Yi became Emperor of China in 1908, at the age of three. Four years later he was removed from his throne by the Republican Revolution. (Burke 470)

Example of Plagiarism #2: Using Another's Ideas

Now read the passage below from the book *They Met at Gettysburg* by Edward J. Stackpole. Take notes on the passage, and then write your own paragraph.

Original Passage

Gettysburg marked the climax of the Confederacy's supreme effort of the war. The Fourth of July, 1863 in retrospect was an Independence Day of vast historic significance, coupling as it did the capitulation of Vicksburg and the failure of Lee's invasion of the North, with all that those two important events were destined to mean for the preservation of the Union.

You must attribute the ideas in this paragraph to the person who wrote it, Edward J. Stackpole. The passage that follows does not do this. It is an example of a plagiarized writing.

Plagiarized Passage

The climax of the Confederacy's supreme Civil War effort occurred at Gettysburg. When Lee's northern invasion failed and the South capitulated at Vicksburg on the Fourth of July in 1863, two events of vast historic significance in the preservation of the Union occurred.

Properly Cited Passage

The climax of the Confederacy's Civil War effort occurred at Gettysburg. When Lee's northern invasion failed and the South capitulated at Vicksburg in 1863, the history books recorded a Fourth of July "of vast historic significance" (Stackpole 321).

A proper citation not only gives credit where it is due, it also refers the reader to the list of works cited found at the end of the paper. The page number tells where the material can be found in the source.

You Have Plagiarized If You . . .

- presented words or ideas as your own that you paraphrased from an unnamed source.
- copied words or ideas from the Internet and pasted them into your paper without attributing them to the Web site and author.
- presented facts from any source without giving the author credit.
- used descriptive phrases from an author without documenting the source.
- handed in someone else's term paper and claimed it as your own.
- had someone else write significant portions of your paper.

What You Don't Have to Cite

Any ideas or opinions that are your own will need no acknowledgment. Common expressions, mottoes, or quotations don't need documentation either. For example, the sayings "A stitch in time saves nine" or "If you can't stand the heat, get out of the kitchen" would need no citation. Information that is common knowledge is also exempt, such as "Abraham Lincoln gave his Gettysburg Address at the dedication of a burial ground for Union soldiers."

If you have trouble deciding whether something you have written may be plagiarism, be safe and document your sources.

Copyrights

One last thing to consider is copyright infringement. If you copy an entire document, or large parts of it, as a handout for a class or to accompany a report, you should receive written permission from the author or publisher. It does not matter whether you find this document in a book, a magazine, or on the Internet. You need the publisher's permission to use this document.

APA Format

If you are writing a term paper for a science or social studies class, your teacher may want you to use the "APA" style. APA stands for American Psychological Association, the organization that established the style. Because behavioral and scientific claims depend upon research and up-to-the-minute documentation, many professionals working in these fields use the APA format as their standard.

The Basic APA Source Card

When writing a source card for most books using the APA format, begin with the author's last name. Follow this with a comma and the author's first and middle initial (if given). Place the year of publication in parentheses, followed by a period. The title of the book appears in italics and only proper nouns and the first letter of the word in the title are capitalized. Then comes the place of publication, a colon, and the publisher's name. This is the standard APA format for writing source cards and cite lists. (See Fig. 21.)

Ogilvy, D. (2004). *Confessions of an advertising man*. London: Southbank.

Fig. 21. Sample source card for a book using APA style.

Additional APA Style for Books

Begin with the author's surname, followed by the author's initials. If the publication is an edited or translated book, indicate that information after the author's name with the abbreviation *Ed.* or *Trans.* in parentheses. Then add the year of publication, in parentheses.

Next, list the title of the book in italics. If a book is a second or later edition, or if it is one volume of a book with multiple volumes, list the edition or volume number using the abbreviations *ed.* or *vol.* in parentheses after the title.

After the title, add the place of publication. For well-known cities such as New York and Boston, simply add a colon after the name of the city. For less well-known cities, identify the state in which the city is located.

Finally, list the name of the publisher, including the words *Books, University, Press*, or *Association*, if those words are part of the name. Do not add the words *Publisher, Company*, or *Inc.*

Crediting Sources in Your Paper

Crediting sources within your report will also be slightly different if you use the APA style. Within the parentheses you must include the author's last name, a comma, the year of publication, a comma, and the page reference (preceded by *p.* or *pp.*).

(Frazier, 2005, pp. 48-55).

APA Style for Articles

Begin with the author's last name, a comma, and the first and middle initial, followed by the copyright date in parentheses. If you are citing an article from a publication that appears monthly, add the month of publication after the year, in parentheses. If the publication appears daily or weekly, add the entire date.

Titles of articles, essays, or book chapters are capitalized in the same way as book titles but are neither put in quotation marks nor italicized. List the journal, magazine, or other source where you found the article and italicize this information. If there is a volume or issue number, add a comma after the name of the periodical and add this information in italics. Follow this with a comma and the page number or numbers.

Frazier, I. (2005, April 25). Invaders: Destroying Baghdad. *New Yorker*, 48-55.

Works Cited

The list below should help you when gathering your works cited page using the APA style. For a more complete guide, refer to a copy of *The Publication Manual of the American Psychological Association* or visit their Web site: http://www.apastyle.org/.

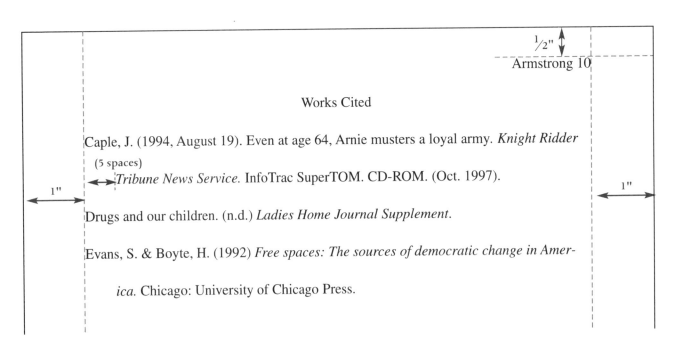

Fig. 20. Model of works cited in APA style.
(Size of page is reduced.)

Fig. 20. Model of works cited in APA style(continued)

Faulkner, W. (1987). *Country lawyer and other stories for the screen.* Eds. Brodsky &

Hamblin. Jackson: University of Mississippi Press.

Frazier, I. (2005, April 25). Invaders: Destroying Baghdad. *New Yorker*, 48-55.

McCabe, L. (1996, April). The Scopes monkey trial—July 10-July 25, 1925. *Inherit the*

wind homepage http://xroads.virginia.edu (Sept. 29, 1997).

Montaigne, M. (1968) Of cannibals. *Utopian literature: A selection.* Ed. J. Johnson.

New York: Modern Library-Random, 134-50.

Solzhenitsyn, A. (1968). *Cancer ward.* New York: Dial.

Solzhenitsyn, A. (1963). *One day in the life of Ivan Denisovich.* New York: Praeger.

½"

1"

1"

All text 1" from bottom of page.

Factors Influencing

the Scopes Trial

by

Indira Singh

American History
10:00 M.-F.
Mr. E. Von der Porten
17 May 2005

Note: This paper is printed on both sides of the pages to save space. You
will use only one side of the page. These pages are reduced in size.

Singh 1

The Teaching of Evolution is Challenged

In 1925, fundamentalists persuaded the Tennessee legislature to pass a bill outlaw-ing the teaching of evolution in that state's public schools. It was a major victory for the fundamentalists. Since they held that the Bible should be taken literally, they believed that God created all the world and its creatures in six 24-hour days. The theory of evolution, which said that the world and nature had developed slowly over millions of years, was repugnant to them.

However, the Tennessee law, known as the Butler Act, did not go unchallenged for long. The act received its first test that same year when John Scopes of Dayton in Rhea County, Tennessee, was arrested for teaching evolution. Technically, the Scopes trial was only supposed to decide whether or not the defendant was guilty of breaking the antievolution law. Yet, William Jennings Bryan, the chief prosecutor, and Clarence Darrow, the chief defense attorney, chose to broaden the basis of the argument. They wished to debate whether the legislature had the right to limit the kinds of theories that could be taught in school. Furthermore, the two men were determined to make the trial a contest between these evolutionary theories and fundamentalism.

Because important issues were at stake, it is worth considering how the attitudes of Rhea County residents affected the outcome of the case.

Aspects of the Trial

From the beginning, the Scopes trial was a staged affair. As soon as the Butler Act went into effect in March of 1925, the American Civil Liberties Union (ACLU) began

searching for a person who would test the antievolution law (Settle 36; Shenkman and

Reiger 326).

The ACLU soon found a willing defendant in John Thomas Scopes, a high school

coach from Dayton, Tennessee. Scopes had substituted as a biology teacher for two

weeks one spring and had reviewed material with the class for final exams. Ironically,

Scopes was not even certain he had included evolution in the review (Ragsdale 35),

though he believed he had (Settle 44).

Once the ACLU was notified of Scopes' intention, they came to his aid with

publicity, money, and a renowned defense team (Settle 45). Yet even as the ACLU swung

into action, fundamentalists began gathering their own forces. ACLU critics did their

best to link the organization with a broad range of un-American activities. This quote

from a committee report of the New York legislature—published on the first day of the

Scopes trial, in the local *Times*—was typical:

> The American Civil Liberties Union, in the last analysis, is a supporter of all
>
> subversive movements, and its propaganda is detrimental to the best interests of the
>
> state. It attempts not only to protect crime, but also to encourage attacks upon our
>
> institutions in every form. (qtd. in Ginger 194)

The *Knoxville Journal* printed this attack and stated further that the ACLU sprang from "the notorious pacifist organizations of wartime fame which were presumably financed by German agents in the country" (qtd. in Ginger 194).

The fundamentalists did not trust their cause to the newspapers alone. On May 13, shortly after the ACLU had chosen the initial team of defense lawyers, politician and fundamentalist William Jennings Bryan volunteered to prosecute the case. The state speedily named him a "special prosecutor." With Bryan's induction, the trial was guaranteed to become a debate over the constitutionality of the Butler Act (Scopes and Presley 66).

Bryan seemed the ideal spokesman for the fundamentalist cause. As a former secretary of state and three-time presidential candidate, he was a famous statesman. Yet Bryan had a reputation for being a small-town man. This, in addition to his dedication to fundamentalism and his gift for speaking, made him very popular with the citizens of Dayton and most of the Bible Belt (Scopes and Presley 209-17).

After Bryan signed on for the prosecution, world-renowned lawyer Clarence Darrow volunteered to defend Scopes. "The atheist lawyer from Chicago," as fundamentalists called him, was readily accepted by the defense (Franklin 298).

With the defendant, prosecutor, and defense now in place, the townspeople began to react to the pending battle. From the start, there was little doubt about which side most citizens of Dayton would favor. The majority of residents were church members (Scopes and Presley 39; Ragsdale 40). In fact, three-fourths of Dayton's social life centered around the church. Further, most Daytonians were fundamentalists "as far as they thought of such matters at all" (de Camp 81).

Daytonians made no secret of their allegiance, although the tone of their expression shifted as the trial approached. At first, Dayton was flooded with "monkey business" remarks and images, especially in advertising. However, after Bryan's arrival, the monkey references were replaced by religious allusions (Scopes and Presley 84).

Initially, Dayton slanted local law to favor the fundamentalists. While Bryan was given a permit to speak on the courthouse lawn, a "Brooklyn modernist" (presumably an evolution advocate) was refused one. Dayton's head commissioner explained that he was concerned the modernist might be attacked. Two days later, Dayton policy changed again. All public preaching permits were denied while the trial lasted (Ginger 100).

Despite the ban, Bible experts and evangelists invaded Dayton to criticize both the trial and the agnostic Scopes. Preachers lectured in the streets, while antievolution crusaders doggedly tried to convert news reporters covering the story (de Camp 163-65).

The fundamentalists found other outlets for their point of view. The Anti-Evolution League set up headquarters downtown and sold fundamentalist literature (Scopes and Presley 98). Even more visible were the many religious signs and banners that could be seen on fences, trees, utility poles, and buildings (de Camp 162). These signs urged people to "Come to Jesus" and warned "Prepare to Meet Thy Maker" (Ragsdale 99).

Other signs declared "We Are Not Apes—We Are Men." The most flagrant banner—

exhorting "Read Your Bible Daily"—was hung in the courtroom, right over the judge

(Scopes and Presley 100; Clark 281). At the defense's request, this banner was

removed.

Given the natural sympathies and prejudicial atmosphere of Rhea County, the

defense knew it would probably be impossible to obtain an unbiased jury. Therefore,

Darrow and his associates agreed to seat several jurors who undoubtedly sympathized

with the fundamentalists (de Camp 209-14). They finally had to settle for a jury

composed of six Baptists, four Methodists, and one Disciple of Christ. Only one juror

did not attend church (Settle 75; Ragsdale 100), though even that juror was from a

Baptist family (Ginger 99). The jurors' local ties were strong too. Five of them had been

born in Rhea County (Ragsdale 100).

The defense faced problems not only with a prejudiced jury but also with a prejudiced

judge. Defense lawyers, evolutionists, and journalists had their doubts about Judge John T.

Raulston's impartiality from the beginning. The fact that he was a lay preacher in the

Methodist Episcopal Church made them particularly skeptical (de Camp 84).

Raulston immediately confirmed suspicions of his prejudice by opening the trial

with a prayer. Wrote defense lawyer Arthur Garfield Hays, it was "not just an ordinary

prayer, but an argumentative one, directed straight at the defense" (qtd. in Larson 150, but other sources indicate differently: de Camp 175-76).

Another one of Judge Raulston's questionable decisions was to excuse the jury during most of the testimony so that it would not "prejudice them." Jurors were told to sit out of hearing range outside the courthouse. The judge seemed to have forgotten that a loudspeaker system was transmitting the trial to a large share of Dayton (de Camp 142).

While Raulston excluded the jury from the trial, he seemed to encourage everyone else to attend. Raulston knew the Scopes case was a publicity magnet. Indeed, reporters from around the world—nearly 200 of them—filed stories from Dayton on a daily basis (Moran 2). Speaking to reporters prior to the trial, the judge commented, "Never any case like it before . . . . They say it's in all the New York papers. Of course they'll appeal it and it'll go to the Supreme Court" (qtd. in Ginger 87).

To foster press attention, Raulston allowed photographers free rein in the courtroom. To be fair to the judge, this was often the fashion at trials during the 1920s (de Camp 175). However, the result was constant interruptions and distractions, which only served to further muddy the proceedings.

Raulston's most crucial means of influencing the trial came when he ruled on the tactics of the defense. Darrow based his case on a two-pronged attack. First, he tried to get Raulston to dismiss the charges against Scopes on the grounds that the Butler Act was unconstitutional. Raulston refused to accept the argument.

Then Darrow attempted to prove evolution was factually true by calling scientific experts to the stand (Ginger 78, 88). Bryan anticipated this strategy. "If we can shut out the expert testimony, which is intended to prevent enforcement of the law, we will be through in a short time," Bryan noted (qtd. in Ginger 80).

Bryan's hopes were fulfilled when Raulston ruled that experts would not be allowed to testify for the defense (Ragsdale 101). However, Raulston had no objection to the expert testimony being read into the record (Settle 95). A disgusted Darrow later called Raulston's role during the trial "campaigning for re-election" (qtd. in Ginger 196).

Stripped of his expert witnesses, Darrow was obliged to turn his attack on Bryan himself by putting the prosecutor on the stand. In the course of a raking examination, Darrow's challenging questions demanded that Bryan choose between his unswerving religious faith and the scientific findings of the day—or answer that he did not know. At different points in the interrogation, Bryan tried all three approaches when answering the questions, but with little success. (Larson 188). Darrow succeeded in making Bryan's fundamentalist beliefs look ridiculous. Some of "the atheist lawyer's" points even won applause from the Bryan supporters who crowded the courtroom (Ragsdale 103).

Yet in the end, Darrow could not win. As the trial drew to a close, Judge Raulston reminded jurors that the issue was whether or not Scopes had taught evolution. Darrow protested, "Your Honor, we are wasting time. You should call the jury and instruct it to bring in a verdict of guilty" (qtd. in Clark 283).

Unfortunately for Scopes, Raulston might as well have done just that. The jury declared the defendant guilty and fined him $100. Scopes told the judge, "Your Honor, I feel that I have been convicted of violating an unjust statute. I will continue in the future . . . to oppose this law in any way I can. Any other action would be in violation of my idea of academic freedom" (qtd. in McCabe).

A Questionable Win for Bryan

Considering all the facts, Darrow's loss was not surprising. In Rhea County, as throughout the Bible Belt, most citizens were fundamentalists. Therefore, people naturally revered the Scopes prosecutor, fundamentalist Bryan. Nor did Bryan stand alone. Fundamentalists offered both verbal and print support of his cause by blasting Scopes, the defense lawyers, the ACLU, and evolution. These propaganda forces succeeded in turning the area around the Dayton courthouse into a circus.

Inside the courtroom, bias was all too evident. The jurors obviously sympathized with the fundamentalists from the start, and the judge seemed less than impartial.

Given this atmosphere and these participants, the outcome of the Scopes trial was a foregone conclusion.

Works Cited

Clark, Ronald W. <u>The Survival of Charles Darwin: A Biography of a Man and an Idea</u>.

New York: Easton, 1991.

de Camp, L. Sprague. <u>The Great Monkey Trial</u>. Garden City: Doubleday, 1968.

Franklin, Charles. <u>World-Famous Trials</u>. New York: Taplinger, 1966.

Ginger, Ray. <u>Six Days or Forever?: Tennessee v. John Thomas Scopes</u>. New York: Oxford

UP, 1981.

Larson, Edward J. <u>Summer for the Gods: The Scopes Trial and America's Continuing

Debate Over Science and Religion</u>. New York: HarperCollins, 1997.

McCabe, Lyndsey. "The Scopes 'Monkey Trial'—July 10, 1925–July 25, 1925." <u>Inherit the

Wind</u> Home Page. Apr. 1996. 29 Mar. 2005 <http://xroads.virginia.edu~UG97/inherit

/1996home.html>.

Moran, Jeffrey P. <u>The Scopes Trial: A Brief History with Documents</u>. New York:

St. Martin's, 2002.

Ragsdale, W. B. "I Remember Three Weeks in Dayton." <u>American Heritage</u> June 1975: 35+.

Scopes, John T., and James Presley. <u>Center of the Storm</u>. New York: Holt, 1967.

Settle, Mary Lee. <u>The Scopes Trial: The State of Tennessee v. John Thomas Scopes</u>. New

York: Watts, 1972.

Shenkman, Richard, and Kurt Reiger. <u>One-Night Stands with American History: Odd,

Amusing, and Little-Known Incidents</u>. New York: Quill, 1982.

Note: MLA style uses underlining rather than italics on the Works Cited page.
Other style manuals such as the *Chicago Manual of Style* call for italics.

Carry Nation:

Why She Fought for Prohibition

by

Laura Kuypers

American History
Period 4
Mr. E. Von der Porten
12 May 2005

Note: This paper is printed on both sides of the pages to save space. You will
use only one side of the page. These pages are reduced in size.

Carry's Destiny

During the 1840s, the term *manifest destiny* was coined. The phrase summarized the popular view that the United States was destined to rule all of North America because its government, economy, and way of life were superior. This philosophy seemed especially suited to parts of the country where a frontier mentality prevailed. Garrard County, Kentucky, was one such area. The typical resident of that region was hard-drinking and violent, yet extremely religious in a fundamentalist sense.

Into this turbulent time and place, Carry Amelia Moore—later Carry Nation— was born in 1846 (Taylor 15-16). In many respects, Nation's later Prohibition crusade was a perfect expression of the aggressive spirit of the era (see Fig. 1). Yet Nation was more than a product of a general trend.

Fig. 1. Antisaloon poster from The Library of Congress.

What personal influences led this Kentucky girl to become the hatchet-swinging leader of the Prohibition movement?

Influences that Shaped Carry Nation

One primary influence on Carry Nation's life and temperament was something over which she had no control: her genetic inheritance. Insanity ran throughout her family history. Her grandmother, an aunt, an uncle, and a first cousin all had mental problems, and most of them were institutionalized at one point in their lives (Furnas 14, 16-17). Nor did Carry herself escape. She died in 1911 of "nervous trouble" (Severn 76).

One other of Carry's relatives is also thought to have shared the malady: her mother. It was stated during Carry's life that her mother believed herself to be Queen Victoria. Everyone—even her family—could see Mrs. Moore only by appointment (Taylor 18). Carry was never honored with such an appointment (Beals 12-13; Kobler 147). Whether Mrs. Moore was really quite so delusional is arguable, but Carry certainly felt neglected, misunderstood, and put upon by her. The relationship between mother and daughter was always very strained. (Grace 24). Carry came to resent being lectured or disciplined by her mother, and she decidedly disliked her mother's fancy dress and flamboyance (Beals 3, 11). Yet this dislike and resentment was mixed with wistfulness. Particularly during her teenage years, Carry seemed to hope for a better relationship with her mother (Beals 24-25).

In order to keep Carry out of her mother's path, Mr. Moore sent Carry to live most of her youth in the slave quarters (Beals 4; Taylor 28-30, 32-33). This environment had a profound influence on Carry. From the household servants, she picked up many super-stitions (Taylor 28-30, 32-33) as well as the habit of stealing (Beals 5; Taylor 33-34). At the same time, she came to believe in the gospel that promised harsh punishment for sins (Beals 6-8, 14; Taylor 35). This latter notion was the foundation for her lifelong religious beliefs. Her adherence to a hellfire-and-brimstone interpretation of the Bible only grew stronger as she matured (Taylor 35).

One event that dramatically strengthened Carry's religious convictions was the result of a childhood illness. Carry came to feel that this illness was punishment for her sins, especially her thievery. This feeling was strengthened by her parents and by at least one minister (Beals 23-25). It was also reinforced by her father's conviction that Carry was going to die. Carry knew her father would deeply mourn her, and she felt overwhelmed by the prospect of his grief. Carry loved and adored her father (Kobler 147). Her relationship with him was compensation for the frustrations she experienced with her mother (Beals 26-27). It was her father's urging that led the ailing girl to go to a revival meeting and to Sunday school. Finally, though still confined to bed, she was carried to an icy river and baptized. Carry eventually recovered from her sickness.

However, the experience at the river remained with her for the rest of her life. It sparked her driving religious zeal (Bales 26-27; Taylor 39, 42-44).

Carry combined her convictions with a determined personality. A grade-school classmate described Carry in the following way:

> She was inclined to be a tom-boy, was very strong-willed and absolutely afraid of nothing. She dominated the school, and was distinctly a leader of both boys and girls . . . . I especially recall the martial spirit, and how she used to delight in assuming the roll [sic] of conqueror. (qtd. in Bader 133)

Her personality grew increasingly headstrong in her late teens, as did her religious views. Those sins that symbolized her earlier life—lying and stealing—she now opposed. Yet Carry could not put her troubled past entirely behind her. Her religious beliefs became mixed with the frequent hallucinations and strange dreams she experienced (Severn 76; Furnas 291). As a result, her brand of Christianity took on an obsessive and unhealthy form.

With adulthood came some severe tests of Carry's faith. Carry met, fell in love with, and married Dr. Charles Gloyd. Unfortunately, Gloyd was an alcoholic (Beals 44-45). When he arrived at the wedding drunk (Taylor 50-54), it was apparent that Carry's love alone would not alter his habits.

Yet, for a time, Carry still clung to that hope (Beals 44-45). When she at last realized that affection was not reforming Gloyd, Carry resorted to following him to the

Masonic lodge where he drank every night. This too proved useless. Finally,

pregnant and close to having a nervous breakdown, she returned to her parents

(Taylor 50-54).

Gloyd died six months later (Furnas 292). However, this did not alleviate Carry's

burden. In fact, Gloyd's death made her feel guilty because she had failed to cure him.

She attempted to stifle this emotion at first by caring for Gloyd's mother. Later she

took a more militant approach by attacking the evils she thought had killed Gloyd—

tobacco, the Masons, and alcohol (Beals 47, 49-50; Kobler 147).

Yet another worry plagued Carry following Gloyd's death. Would Gloyd's

drinking and her own gloom during her pregnancy taint her child? Her worst fears

seemed to be coming true when the child, Charlien, developed an ulcer in her cheek

while still young (Kobler 149). The ulcer, which caused Charlien's jaws to lock and

left her unable to speak, was almost fatal. The horror of this situation led Carry to

conclude that liquor could cause terrible disabilities (Beals 59).

Eventually a successful operation helped Charlien recover. Yet Carry remained

sorrowful. She felt Charlien was still marked by Gloyd's sin. Carry's opinion was only

reconfirmed when Charlien later rejected the church and its beliefs (Beals 64, 68).

Then, following her own marriage, Charlien became an alcoholic (Beals 106) and was institutionalized more than once for mental problems (Kobler 149; Taylor 58).

While Charlien was experiencing these problems, Carry learned that Gloyd's mother had died and that her own mother had been placed in an asylum (Beals 81-84). These tragedies added to Carry's burden of guilt.

At last in 1877, Carry found the symbol of purpose for which she had been unconsciously searching. That year Carry was married again, this time to David Nation. Her new name, Carry A. Nation, rang with meaning to her. It seemed to reveal God's plan for her: she was intended to wage a war against liquor and other evils (Kobler 146-47). She also found her initials, C.A.N., meaningful. They suggested Carry was destined to succeed on her crusade (Severn 77; Taylor 62). She now felt assured that whatever she said or did had God's approval (Beals 70, 74-76).

At first Carry's battle against liquor was moderate and lawful. She visited jailed drunkards and urged abstinence. However, her approach changed when she grasped the scope of the drinking problem. Although Kansas, where she and David then lived, was legally a "dry" state, the unlawful sale of liquor was not prosecuted. Carry came to believe that the only way the law could be enforced was through direct radical action (Beals 81-84). Since to her, selling liquor was illegal, any business that sold liquor was therefore outside the protection of the law (McHenry 299).

Satisfied with her own logic and the sanctity of her convictions, Carry began her famous hatchet-swinging, saloon-smashing war to abolish alcohol (Severn 78-79). John

Kobler reports that she didn't just confine herself to a hatchet. "At various times she also

used her fists, rocks, brickbats, a sledgehammer, an iron bar, prayer and invective"

(146). At long last, the pent-up guilt and aggression stemming from Carry's stressful

childhood were being vented in glorious fury (Beals 51-52).

During the rest of her life, Carry "continued to attack Masonry, to grab cigarettes

and cigars from smokers, to make fun of people with fine clothing, to advocate women's

suffrage, and to fight the liquor interests." She battled alcohol abuse around the

Midwest, on both coasts of the United States, and in England and Canada. Her crusade

ended only when old age forced her to retire to a farm in Arkansas (carry5.htm).

Inspired by Guilt

Carry Nation was raised in a stormy environment that left a lasting and probably

unhealthy impression on her. In religion she found the purpose and assurances she

desperately needed to resolve the conflicts of her childhood. Yet, affected by hereditary

mental problems, Carry's religious convictions became extreme and obsessive. They

also compounded her guilt, leaving her feeling at least partly responsible for the deaths

of her husband and mother-in-law, as well as for her mother's and daughter's problems.

This guilt was an overwhelming burden for Carry. To relieve it, she unconsciously searched for a cause to which she could devote herself. Her first husband's drinking

problem and her second husband's name were all the inspiration she needed. Family

troubles, mental instability, and religious beliefs; such were the factors behind Carry

Nation's "manifest destiny."

Works Cited

Bader, Robert Smith. <u>Prohibition in Kansas: A History</u>. Lawrence: UP of Kansas, 1986.

Beals, Carleton. <u>Cyclone Carry</u>. Philadelphia: Chilton, 1962.

"Carry A. Nation." 29 Apr. 2005 <http//www.kshs.org/exhibits/carry/carry5.htm>.

Furnas, J.C. <u>The Late Demon Rum</u>. New York: Putnam, 1965.

Grace, Fran. <u>Carry A. Nation: Retelling the Life</u>. Bloomington: Indiana UP, 2001.

Kobler, John. <u>Ardent Spirits: The Rise and Fall of Prohibition</u>. Philadelphia:

    Da Capo, 1993.

McHenry, Robert, ed. <u>Liberty's Women</u>. Springfield: Merriam, 1980.

Severn, Bill. <u>The End of the Roaring Twenties: Prohibition and Repeal</u>. New York:

    Messner, 1975.

Taylor, Robert Lewis. <u>Vessel of Wrath</u>. New York: NAL, 1966.

Appendix 2
Margin and Spacing Diagrams: Handwritten

Handwritten First Page (No Title Page)
all copy is double-spaced

Kuypers 1 — last name and page number placed ½" from top of page

Laura Kuypers — your name on first full line, class information, and date

Mr. E. Von der Porten

American History, Period 4

12 May 2005

Carry Nation: Why She Fought for Prohibition — title centered

— 1 blank line

Carry's Destiny — section title centered

— 1 blank line

During the 1840s, the term <u>manifest destiny</u> was coined. — indented ½"

The phrase summarized the popular view that the United States

was destined to rule all of North America because its government, — 1" right margin / 1" left margin

economy, and way of life were superior. This philosophy seemed

especially suited to parts of the country where a frontier mentality

prevailed. Garrard County, Kentucky, was one such area. The

typical resident of that region was hard-drinking and violent, yet

extremely religious in a fundamentalist sense.

Into this turbulent time and place, Carry Amelia Moore—

later Carry Nation—was born in 1846 (Taylor 15-16). In many

respects, Nation's later Prohibition crusade was a perfect

— 3 or 4 blank lines

Handwritten Title Page
center all lines

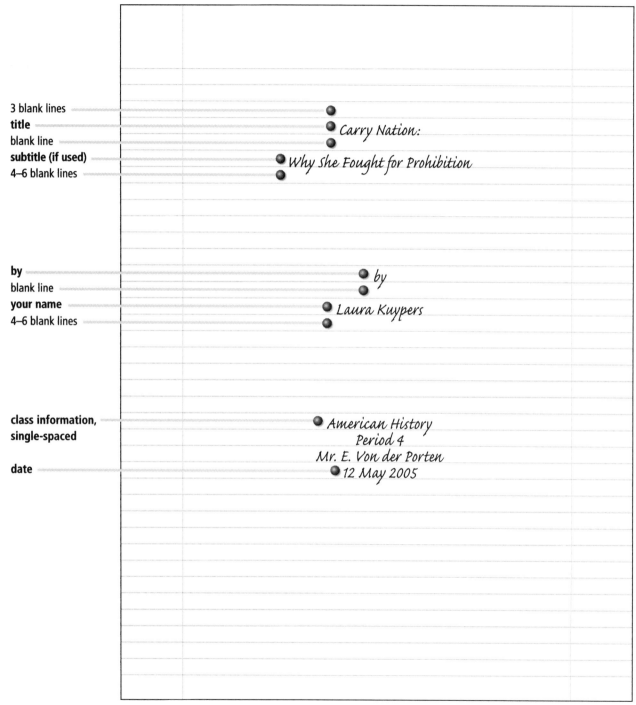

3 blank lines

title — *Carry Nation:*

blank line

subtitle (if used) — *Why She Fought for Prohibition*

4–6 blank lines

by — *by*

blank line

your name — *Laura Kuypers*

4–6 blank lines

class information, single-spaced — *American History*
Period 4
Mr. E. Von der Porten

date — *12 May 2005*

Note: If your teacher requires a title page, follow this model.

Handwritten Works Cited
works cited is double-spaced

Kuypers 10 ●························ **last name and page number placed ½" from top of page**

Works Cited ●·························· **section title centered on first full line**

●·························· 1 blank line

Bader, Robert Smith. *Prohibition in Kansas: A History*. Lawrence:

●·························· indented ½"

UP of Kansas, 1986.

●·························· 1" left margin
●·························· 1" right margin

Beals, Carleton. *Cyclone Carry*. Philadelphia: Chilton, 1962. ●

"Carry A. Nation." 29 Apr. 2005 <http//www.kshs.org/exhibits/

carry/carry5.htm>.

Furnas, J.C. *The Late Demon Rum*. New York: Putnam, 1965.

Grace, Fran. *Carry A. Nation: Retelling the Life*.

Bloomington: Indiana UP, 2001.

Kobler, John. *Ardent Spirits: The Rise and Fall of Prohibition*.

Philadelphia: Da Capo, 1993.

McHenry, Robert, ed. *Liberty's Women*. Springfield: Merriam,

1980.

Severn, Bill. *The End of the Roaring Twenties: Prohibition and

Repeal*. New York: Messner, 1975.

Taylor, Robert Lewis. *Vessel of Wrath*. New York: NAL, 1966.

●·························· 3 or 4 blank lines

Appendix 3
Margin and Spacing Diagrams: Typewritten

Typewritten First Page (No Title Page)
all copy is double-spaced

Singh 1

Indira Singh
Mr. E. Von der Porten
American History, 10:00 M-F
17 May 2005

Factors Influencing the Scopes Trial

Introduction

    In 1925, fundamentalists persuaded the Tennessee legislature to pass a bill outlawing the teaching of evolution in that state's public schools. It was a major victory for the fundamentalists. Since they held that the Bible should be taken literally, they believed that God created all the world and its creatures in six 24-hour days. The theory of evolution, which said that the world and nature had developed slowly over millions of years, was repugnant to them.

    However, the Tennessee law, known as the Butler Act, did not go unchallenged for long. The act received its first test that same year when John Scopes of Dayton in Rhea County, Tennessee, was arrested for teaching evolution. Technically, the Scopes trial was only supposed to decide whether or not the defendant was guilty of breaking the antievolution law. Yet, William Jennings Bryan, the chief prosecutor, and Clarence Darrow, the chief defense attorney, chose to broaden the basis of the argument. They wished to debate whether the legislature had the right to limit the kinds of theories that could be taught in school. Furthermore, the two men were determined to make the trial a contest between evolutionary theories and fundamentalism.

Callouts:
- last name and page number placed ½" from top of page
- your name 1" from top of page, class information, and date
- title
- blank line
- section title centered
- 5 indented spaces
- 1" left margin
- 1" right margin
- 1" from bottom of page

Typewritten Title Page
center all lines

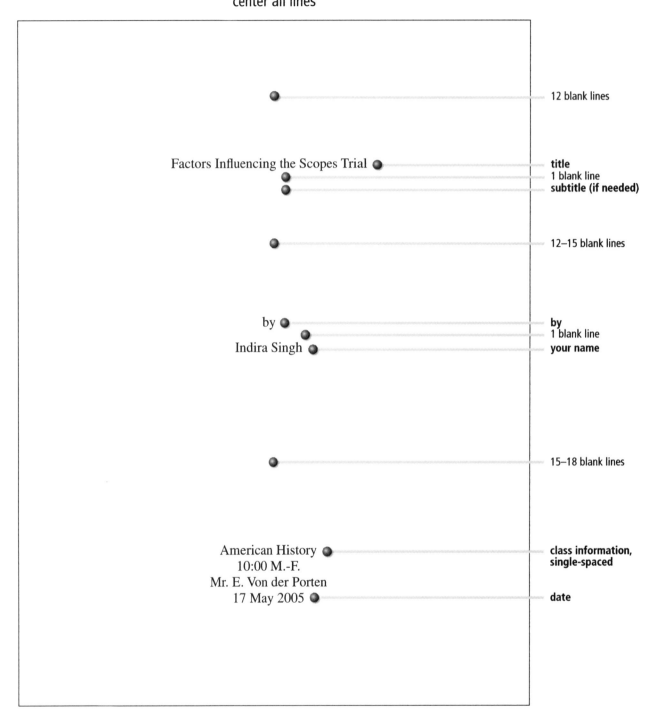

12 blank lines

Factors Influencing the Scopes Trial — **title**
1 blank line
subtitle (if needed)

12–15 blank lines

by — **by**
1 blank line
Indira Singh — **your name**

15–18 blank lines

American History — **class information, single-spaced**
10:00 M.-F.
Mr. E. Von der Porten
17 May 2005 — **date**

Typewritten Works Cited
works cited is double-spaced

Singh 9

Works Cited

Clark, Ronald W. The Survival of Charles Darwin: A Biography of a Man and

an Idea. New York: Easton, 1991.

de Camp, L. Sprague. The Great Monkey Trial. Garden City: Doubleday, 1968.

Franklin, Charles. World-Famous Trials. New York: Taplinger, 1966.

Ginger, Ray. Six Days or Forever?: Tennessee v. John Thomas Scopes. New

York: Oxford UP, 1981.

Larson, Edward J. Summer for the Gods: The Scopes Trial and America's

Continuing Debate Over Science and Religion. New York:

HarperCollins, 1997.

McCabe, Lyndsey. "The Scopes 'Monkey Trial'—July 10, 1925–July 25,

1925." Inherit the Wind Home Page. Apr. 1996. 29 Mar. 2005

<http://xroads.virginia.edu~UG97/inherit/1996home.html>.

Moran, Jeffrey P. The Scopes Trial: A Brief History with Documents. New

York: St. Martin's, 2002.

Ragsdale, W. B. "I Remember Three Weeks in Dayton." American Heritage

June 1975: 35+.

Scopes, John T., and James Presley. Center of the Storm. New York: Holt, 1967.

Settle, Mary Lee. The Scopes Trial: The State of Tennessee v. John Thomas

Scopes. New York: Watts, 1972.

Shenkman, Richard, and Kurt Reiger. One-Night Stands with American

History: Odd, Amusing, and Little-Known Incidents. New York: Quill,

1982.

Index